AMBASSADORS FOR CHRIST

with love
Kim

Dave
& Hannah
(+ Bump!)

'We are therefore Christ's ambassadors,
as though God were making his appeal through us.'
(2 Cor. 5:20)

Ambassadors for Christ

Personal testimonies to God's healing presence

Edited by Kathleen O'Sullivan SSL

Hodder & Stoughton
LONDON SYDNEY AUCKLAND

British Library Cataloguing in Publication Data
A record for this book is available form the British Library

ISBN 0 340 67891 7

Typeset by Hewer Text Composition Services, Edinburgh
Printed and bound in Great Britain by
Cox & Wyman Ltd, Reading, Berks

Hodder and Stoughton Ltd
A Division of Hodder Headline PLC
338 Euston Road
London NW1 3BH

To the Blessed Trinity:
God the Father who created us,
God the Son who redeemed us,
God the Holy Spirit who teaches us the meaning of love.

CONTENTS

ACKNOWLEDGMENTS

The dedication of this book reveals who was really behind it and whose praises for making it possible need most of all to be sung. But human agency was very necessary to its successful conclusion. Many people have given freely of their time and expertise to make it happen. In particular, I must single out Dee Dannatt for her constant patience, her support, her careful typing and her expert sorting and storing of data; Dr Tony White for allowing me extravagant access to his fax machine for outgoing and incoming messages; Eilish Heath for her unwavering support and her listening heart; and John Morrill for helping me and several of the authors to find the right words to communicate to others their intimate encounters with God, and for his help in putting the little autobiographies into some sort of standard shape. Above all, I want to acknowledge the generosity, the humility and the trust of the twenty-eight authors who reached inner depths and allowed themselves in many cases to be sent deeper still. Their willingness to tell their stories is a great service to a Loving God and a wounded Church.

My sincere thanks to Hodder and Stoughton for

their unfailing courtesy and most especially to the religious books editor, Elspeth Taylor, whose keen insights, empathy and openness to suggestions were refreshing and rewarding.

The views expressed by the contributors are theirs alone and do not necessarily reflect the views of the editor.

Kathleen O'Sullivan SSL

INTRODUCTION

Kathleen O'Sullivan

This book is more than a collection of stories about God's work in the lives of his people.

It is a **love-response** to their God who is alive, real and continuously holding them close – while leaving them free to choose (or not to choose) his plans.

It is a **faith-response** from believers who have paused to discover the presence of God in their lives, active at this very moment within them, caring for them even at times when it may seem they are lost.

It is a **hope-response** to the God who is their strength and their rock; a God who fulfils his promises; a God who transforms, even our worst failures in life, when we trust him and listen to his voice.

In this book, you will find contributors of different Christian denominations, men and women, young and old, clergy, religious and lay people.

You will find genuine accounts of the discovery in prayer and reflection that each person finds he or she is unique and truly loved by God.

This is 'holy ground', where writers share their deepest truth about who they are and long to be for the God they believe in; they reveal, in a variety of ways, who God is for them.

These writers have heard the voice of God inviting them to be still and to know him: 'Today if you hear his voice, harden not your hearts' (Ps. 94:8). They have been truly obedient. In this way they have become ambassadors for Christ (2 Cor. 5:20).

It has been a costly venture for the writers. It takes a lot of prayer, of listening, and of being open to the Spirit, to ensure that the focus remains on God and not on oneself. It takes courage to share one's inner self even with close friends; to do so here with unknown, unseen readers who may not empathise, calls for compelling motivation.

The motivation is simple but deep. **We are the Church.** That truth we are familiar with, but surely the time has come for us to stand up and be counted. This was the voice of the Lord which I seemed to hear, but its confirmation lay in its resounding in the hearts of God's people. The writers heard, they recognised God's voice and responded with incredible generosity.

'How can we repay the Lord for all His goodness to us?' awoke in us an answer of *'a life for a life'* – meaning that Jesus Christ had given his life that we may live. It seems therefore right and fitting, at a time when so many reject the humanity and divinity of the Lord Jesus, that we, Christians, bear witness to our **personal life-experience**: sinners though we undoubtedly are, the love and the power of the Lord Jesus Christ can transform lives. Our lives are in the process of being thus transformed. This is our story.

Christ is the head and we are the body of the Church. If our love for Christ is real, then we must love the **whole Christ**, since every member is a brother or sister in his body. In the life-experiences, shared here in faith, Christ's presence is manifested frequently through timely help from a brother or sister. Indeed 'we have freely received, we must now freely give'. Christ has empowered others to help us. It is our turn now. This is our motivation. We hope that our 'laying down our lives' – even in this simple way – may help someone else out there. We become Christ's ambassadors when we live truly in the power of Christ alive within us. By our dying for one another – empowered by the love of Jesus – the **Church of Christ will live**.

Thus the voice of the Lord, heard in an individual heart, will resound from the mountain tops when it is taken up and answered now by one ambassador, now by another, fulfilling Christ's own prayer to his Father: 'that they may be one, as we are one' (John 17:22).

LOVE

The life-experience mysteries which are offered in this section reveal many aspects of love.

Because the concept of love today is too often debased, it is refreshing and inspiring to see genuine love being highlighted. Invariably, such love implies selfless giving; the grain of wheat must die so that another may live, that the harvest may indeed be abundant.

However, love, faith and hope form a little trinity – like the three persons in the one God. The emphasis in this section falls on love, yet where there is genuine love, there is a living faith and hope that springs eternal. The 'love-experience' is strongly supported by the presence of hope and faith. As in matters spiritual, so in the human dimension – God's gift to us – we human individuals need the support of one another. Hence our assembling together, to pray, to worship as the body of Christ.

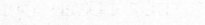

THE FLOODED SOUL

John Morrill

John Morrill is reader in early modern history in the University of Cambridge and vice-master of Selwyn College. He writes extensively, mainly about the seventeenth century. He was received into the Catholic Church in 1977 and ordained to the permanent married diaconate in 1996. He has four daughters.

This testimony of John, a church-going teenager, who in his twenties experienced spiritual bereftness and desolation, is gripping. In God's time, John came, in adulthood, to the unutterable joy of rediscovering God's love flooding his soul and suffusing the whole world. This is a truly inspiring story of the love of God transforming darkness into the light of his abiding presence.

K.O'S.

I was brought up in a prayerful and believing family and after my (Anglican) confirmation at the age of fifteen I

5

was an altar server and Sunday School teacher. I 'went to church' most weeks until I was about twenty and then began to drift. Increasingly in the later 1960s, I intellectualised God, seeking to *understand* him and I was drawn into the liberal 'death of God' theology. Such personal relationship as I thought I had with him – in fact with the glorified Son and never the Father – evaporated as I talked earnestly about the 'ground-of-being'. Supposedly a liberation from a tired, limiting notion of God-as-bearded-paternalist-in-the-sky, actually it was a locking of the gates of the heart and a closing of the frontiers of my mind to all but a few abstract ideas.

For seven years I abandoned anything that could be called a personal relationship with God. I could not pray – at least in any way I could recognise as prayer – and I felt angry and empty if I attended acts of worship. I was angry because I could sense a God *outside* myself, but could not find him *within* myself. Sometimes this caused me great distress. Once on a Sunday morning, sitting in a country cottage, I heard the bells of the medieval parish church calling the faithful to prayer as it had for hundreds of years; and I sat quietly weeping at my inability to answer the call of those bells. And on another Sunday morning I wept much more bitter tears as I listened to Elgar's *Dream of Gerontius* and felt an overwhelming sense of desolation at my inability to assent to the words of the priest at the moment of Gerontius's death (*Proficescere, anima Christiana, de hoc mundo* – 'Go forth upon thy journey Christian soul! Go from this world! Go in the name of God . . . '). It was an affirmation I yearned to make and could not.

In those years I used to go occasionally to see Fr

Geoffrey Preston of the Oxford Dominican House. He listened and said little. He must have sensed that it was playing with words that had got me into this mess and that more words would not get me out of it. He never tried to convince me of anything. He did not counter my complaints against the God-behind-the-clouds. He simply listened, and his quiet acceptance of me as and where I was gave me some kind of relief from the spasms (and they were only spasms) of misery (really self-pity).

Then in Holy Week 1977, when I was thirty-one and Geoffrey was forty-one, he died. I went to his funeral in Leicester where he had recently become prior. The church was packed, and the requiem was concelebrated by all his brethren. And suddenly, I saw something so obvious that I could not believe that I had not seen it before. I recognised that what had drawn me back again and again to Geoffrey was not just Geoffrey, but what shone through him: what he *represented*. The Spirit that radiated from him suffused the whole church. There and then, at the epicentre of that Mass, the doors of my heart that I had kept so tightly closed for years burst *inwards* and the love of God flooded in, overwhelmed me. It felt as though a dam had burst and a torrent of water had flooded parched soil. My soul was inundated by love.

In the twenty years since, God has never been absent from my life. Sometimes, when I have been a faithful Lenten person, I have experienced echoes of that emptiness in that terrifying time between the stripping of the altars on Maundy Thursday and the Easter vigil Mass when all sacraments are suspended and we are reminded of an unredeemed world. Much more powerful was an experience I had when I was in Cracow in 1991 at a conference debating how best to structure Catholic education in post-Communist Eastern Europe. One day 150 or so of us went to Auschwitz. The concentration camp was bad enough, with those dismal sheds, one crammed full of shoes, another with spectacles, another with baby clothes. It was a terrible reminder of man's inhumanity to man. Yet such places have existed somewhere in the world in every century. The experience did not prepare me for Birkenau, the extermination camp. It is largely levelled, more like one of those picturesque medieval sites where one has to imagine the abbey or castle that once stood there from the fragments of masonry and stone pushing up through the soil.

We walked dumb around it, covered as it always is by the lowering clouds of pollution from a local chemical works. It was a place where all true values were inverted. We stopped where Birkenau's intended victims spilled out from the darkness of the cattle trucks into the light. We stopped again where they were divided into groups – those destined for slave labour, those for medical experimentation, those for death. We stopped again where they were stripped of their clothes, of their dignity, of their hope. We stopped again where the sweet-smelling trees had hidden the ovens of death. Fourteen times we stopped, and at every point we were made to recognise how at that place every intellectual gift of God to humanity had been abused to make possible the efficient degradation and destruction of millions of lives. At every spot, we stopped and we prayed a station of the cross. We could barely mumble our responses. None of us spoke at all for an hour afterwards, and none tried to articulate what it had meant to him or her for another twenty-four hours. Then each tried to put it into words.

And I could only say that I had not experienced at that dreadful place the presence of evil (as once I sensed it at a witchcraft museum near Tintagel) but that I had experienced the absence of God. It was, for *me*, a God-forsaken spot. What terrified me was that there I felt *outside* myself those feelings of bereftness which in my desert years I had experienced *within* myself. As Peter momentarily lost trust as he walked on the water, so I momentarily lost trust that God would keep the doors of my heart closed against the vacuum of love without; that his love might ebb away. It didn't happen. But it was a glimpse of how the world might have been without the cross and the Resurrection.

The obverse of the Auschwitz experience, of course, is that some places and some people are suffused with the love of God. And if I have glimpsed what an unredeemed world might be like, I have much more often recognised what a redeemed world *is*. I have been shown signs of God's presence in the world in and through those who are suffused by his love and how that redemptive work is constantly extending and deepening. Finding God in the world is like finding minerals in the earth. Minerals are everywhere, but sometimes they are buried deep and have to be excavated at great cost of effort and time. But often they are on the surface of the earth, where they can be gathered up almost casually. It is there wherever people have prayed and witnessed to their faith year in and year out. Their prayer impregnates the air and the soil. And it is there wherever God reveals himself in the sacramental signs. In the Eucharist we scoop up the living Christ with our bare hands, as easily as we can scoop up ore in an open-cast mine.

I have felt the tangible presence of God – sometimes

Father, sometimes Son and sometimes Holy Spirit – in many situations. At a deathbed, at a Mass in a prison, in a boat on the Sea of Galilee, in the presence of two truly holy persons, by the fireplace in Caiaphas's house where Jesus, just feet away on a winding stair, looked across as Peter denied him. But I have never felt his presence so strongly as in China in 1988. On a holiday (and in holiday mood) after a historical congress, I visited a Buddhist monastery away from the main tourist route. It was on top of a steep hill a few miles outside Suzhou. The hillside was thronged with pilgrims – young men carrying the old on their shoulders up the winding track, old men clawing their way up. To get to the path, I had to run the gauntlet of two rows of beggars, and in a futile attempt to get them to unblock my way, I bought a stick of incense. Already there was an extraordinary intensity to everything – colour, smell, silence. As we reached the top of the hill, the pilgrims seemed to fall away. There was a profound stillness, unbroken by the chattering of birds. I fell mute and then commented seemingly inconsequentially to my companion, a Chinese lecturer, on how beautiful the birdsong was. He was an atheist, brought up to believe that the monks were drones and the monasteries rank superstition. At that moment he burst into tears and said, 'They feed the birds better than they feed themselves.' It was an inadequate way of expressing his encounter with the mystery of the presence of God, but that was what it was. The same God was revealing himself to both of us. I fell on my knees, threw my incense into the burner and prayed with an intensity quite beyond anything I had or have since experienced. I did not offer prayer. It was drawn out of me and yet was instantly replenished within me. I saw that the God who sent his

Son to die for us to show the depths of his love for us was not a God who could be confined to the Catholic faith that I hold and teach. This was pure paradox. This was that God who has revealed himself in Christ, and he was and he is also the God of and for those who know not the Lord Jesus. I still do not know what to make of God's revelation of himself to me in Suzhou. But he was and is the same God who broke down those stubbornly defended doors in my heart in Leicester in 1977 and who calls me always to service and to love.

LETTERS FROM HOME

Dee Dannatt

Dee Dannatt is personal assistant to the principal of a secondary school and lives in Ely with her daughter and husband, who is the warden of a diocesan retreat house. Dee was assistant warden for three years, having previously been involved in parish development work. She is still actively involved in the leading of retreats and quiet days, including Light out of Darkness programmes, and is a Benedictine oblate with the Holy Cross Convent at Rempstone.

Journeying into the past through Scripture allows Dee to be taught by a God of love and tenderness. A sensitive child, Dee had picked up a lot about 'loving God and loving his people' from Christian neighbours. As a fully-fledged member of the Anglican Church, she strove to give God everything, to be 'all things to all people'. Eventually she learned that he wanted her to cease striving too hard, and just to love and trust him! Thus she regained her natural gift of 'lightheartedness' in him – his special love-gift to her. This has empowered her to love God and his people even more deeply.

K.O'S.

St Augustine refers to the Scriptures as our 'letters from home'. This became a reality for me when I recognised that God, whom I so loved, was using the Scriptures in his role as a loving Father who sought to reprimand, cajole, encourage, teach, nurture and love this often striving, over-conscientious, hyperactive child of His. Being 'taught by God' in this way has often been a painful, drawn-out process – going, like Moses, 'into the darkness where God is', to have the 'treasures of darkness' unveiled, as well as walking into the light to encounter the one who is truth, the truth which always ultimately sets me free. Yet, I can trust this loving Father upon whom my upbringing depends, assured that he will always be there to bathe my grazed knees when I fall, to share in my joys and successes, and to allow me to grow into the freedom and fullness of life he earnestly desires for me.

As with all treasured letters they are stored carefully and re-read frequently. Two of the 'letters from home' are stored securely in my heart, so indelibly were they inscribed there. Both are to be found in the Book of Revelation (coincidentally in letter form) and both arrived unexpectedly. The first launched me into a retrospective journey, showing me how far from home I had unwittingly strayed. The second will now always be the means by which he beckons me home, with clear directions for each and every leap or foot-fall.

A long way from Home

The launch into the past was heralded with unmistakable clarity and timeliness, through the letter to Ephesus (Rev. 2:2ff). He told me how he knew my works, my toil and my patient endurance. He knew I had persevered with patience, had suffered for his sake . . ., but yet he had this against me: I had abandoned the love I had at first. These words were so piercing that I could do no other than acknowledge them as being written for me (like Ephesus, a *loveless* church) and my response could only be to repent. Through repentance came instant forgiveness from God with greeting arms stretched wide; while my own heart remained – as yet – unforgiving of myself. And so, there followed the long and arduous process of learning, seeking to understand his lovingly delivered scolding of my hardened heart.

Past events were patiently shown to me – clarifying how I had once loved, but had unintentionally gone astray. I had always been a sensitive child, and although safe and secure in a loving family, I had an indescribable sense of never quite knowing where I belonged beyond the garden gate. My first recollection of church, for instance, was by accompanying my school-friend's family who were regular churchgoers. I watched everyone go to the altar to receive this mysterious bread and wine, leaving me on my knees and bewildered in the back pew, not even having been invited to go for a blessing.

My family, though not churchgoers, were (as I look back with more wisdom) people who *lived* the gospel – people who attended conscientiously to their Nazareth, who coped with their Calvary and who quietly appreciated the joy of Resurrection. I remember, too, people like 'Aunty' Nelly, our next-door neighbour; a bedridden devout Christian with whom I spent hours each day at the age of three, plaiting her hair, wading through her knitting patterns or peeping into the little leather case beneath her bed which contained a tiny communion set. People like her must have prayed so intently for me, and I am sure it was through such unassuming prayerful people that I came to love as I first did. This must have been how – without even being a member of a church – I grew up feeling drawn to intercessory prayer (while being totally unaware of what 'intercession' meant). I would simply and naturally feel compelled, before falling asleep at night, to pray for every marginalised and burdened set of people I could think of. Yet, I remained a non-churchgoer until my late twenties when my husband and I became fully-fledged members of the Anglican Church.

From this recollection, the Lord revealed incidents where 'love' had been the natural keynote in our lives – love for him and for his people, in times of joy and intense sadness. It was in the particularly painful times that we, as 'infant Christians', turned instinctively towards Christ – like little lambs in the thunder and lightning, keeping their gaze upon their shepherd and not upon the storm. Our Shepherd always brought us to the eye of the storm to encounter in that stillness the peace which passes all understanding. In this way, the Lord showed me again 'the love I had at first'. It was an unstriving love which, when one particular storm had ceased, prompted us to offer ourselves to God for full-time ministry (whatever that meant), desiring simply to be with God for people and with people for God. God honoured our willingness to serve him, and within a few months we found ourselves living in a totally new environment, a diocesan retreat house (where, some eight years later, we still seek to serve him).

So how did I eventually abandon this love I had at first? We had launched into servanthood with great enthusiasm and, in some ways, great naivety. Our expectations of ourselves had always been high; we were renowned for 'never doing anything by halves'. It came as some surprise to encounter the mechanics of 'Church' at such close quarters, stalking what was for us the uncharted networks of the Church as an institution, with denominational differences, varying churchmanship, empire building, politics, spiritual élitism. I remember being so devastated listening to a group of Christians who seemed far more impressed by a particular theologian than by Jesus Christ. I felt so disappointed for him. Could we not all see that we were not just breaking his law; we were also breaking his heart? Wherever was God in all of this? Gradually, I recognised him again in those who showed humility, in those who, genuinely sought the Giver rather than the gifts, in those prepared to decrease in order for our Lord to increase. Unwittingly, however, I had fallen into traps myself. As my compassion for people became masked by disillusion, and as I became overwhelmed by our collective sinfulness and strivings, I could no longer recognise the inherent goodness which we also share, which gives integrity to our struggle. Also, as I was unexpectedly drawn into ministries which I had never, in my shyness, envisaged, I began to strive, to ensure that I was adequately equipped! I could not let God or his people down. I strove to wipe out my 'ego', but ignored the 'selfhood' which God had given me. I strove to be all things to all people. I strove as a disciple, mother, wife, daughter, listener, retreat-giver, and child of God. I began to analyse more than reflect. I began to study more than pray. Although affirmed by others, I could never reach the impossible targets I set for myself and was doused liberally in guilt and self-doubt. It was as if I became obsessed to prove how much I loved him, instead of just trusting him. I would constantly say, 'Lord, bind me to your cross, lest I waste all and cause you further pain.'

The scene of Gethsemane, the Agony in the Garden, had always been important to me but it became too intensified; it became unbearable to think of Jesus so isolated at such an agonising time, while his friends slept. I inwardly condemned anything which prevented us from staying awake with the Lord. I now recognise all these traps into which many unsuspecting disciples fall; for only God grades the pilgrimage, and he desires in us a balance between self-denial and self-affirmation. I recognise that it is all too easy to become over-preoccupied with having a ministry, that all this can lead to over-activity, even burn-out, and an over-indulgence in 'self' for whatever reason. Whether one is over-confident or lacking in self-esteem, the outcome is the same – 'self' ends up centre-stage instead of God.

Where had my lightheartedness gone in all of this? It was summed up for me in Ramon Lull's *Lover and the Beloved*: 'Which think you was greater, her sorrow or her joy? And was her joy greater when she saw her Beloved honoured, than her sorrow at seeing Him despised?' I realised that in trying too hard, and in despairing how we all 'missed the mark', Gethsemane had become my home. 'Gethsemane' – the 'crushing' place – had made me so weary that my constant murmurings throughout the day of 'I love you,

Lord' were becoming too muted by anxiety for others to hear.

Showing me the way back Home
Until my strivings ceased and I could do no other than hand over this barrenness to him, there was no possibility of his bringing me back home. He could only keep writing to me, often long-distance, inviting me out of the crushing place and into the place he had destined for me and for all of us.

Thus it was that another unexpected 'letter from home' arrived (Rev. 3:7ff): 'I have set before you an open door . . . I will write on you the name of my God and the name of the city of my God – New Jerusalem.' This affirmed the words from a song I had heard, that the life-giving tomb was awaiting the rebirth of a child, 'New Jerusalem'. And so the adventure began, the rebirth, and the comforting assurance that our Lord will be with his little one through all her growing pains – for this name will take a lifetime to grow into. The meaning of it unfolds gradually and I glimpse the enormity of it, knowing that it is not a name which I cling to for myself; it is a name which marks me, identifies me as belonging everywhere instead of nowhere, a name I share with all his loved ones. The Canticle of New Jerusalem helps me to ponder this vocation: 'You will call your walls Salvation, and your gates Praise . . . the Lord will be your everlasting light, your God will be your splendour.'

It brought me full circle back to the beginning, but at a deeper level of experience, back to loving God and to loving people. I asked him what he would most desire of his New Jerusalem. He asked of me obedience, love, praise, worship, prayerfulness; to be his indwelling guided by him alone; to surrender instead of striving to give him freedom of my inner city, where the fruits of the Spirit may grow in peace and harmony, friendship and forgiveness. 'Worship the Lord, O Jerusalem!' and see how 'the wastelands of Jerusalem break forth with joy'.

One of the blessings of having lived in the retreat house over the past eight years is the privilege of never having become shackled by a particular label or denomination or style of worship. Freedom to explore the rich ecumenical diversities has saved us from putting on dogmatic strait-jackets which so often bind us. In such a setting, the gates of New Jerusalem could be flung open, readily acknowledging that the Lord was to lead this Anglican back home to meet his mother, Mary, the mother of Jesus. St Bonaventure said: 'Go up, therefore, spiritual Mary, no longer into the hill country but into the dwelling place of the spiritual Jerusalem . . . and there before the throne of the eternal Trinity and undivided Unity, humbly kneel in spirit; presenting your Son to God the Father.' We are all called to be mothers to him, enthroning him in our hearts, just like Mary who could not have conceived him in the womb if she had not first conceived him in her heart.

The life of Mary, who nurtured the bread of 'the little ones', has much to say to me about my own life; about womanhood, motherhood, sisterhood; about humility, simplicity, discipleship and ministry. By reflecting upon Mary, my focus is never taken away from Jesus. I see Mary now as a gift from Jesus, a final earthly deed: giving his mother to John, his beloved disciple, and thereby to each of us. Icons of Mary and child remind me that, for Mary, the emphasis is upon Jesus and upon his people. An icon of Mary provides me with a window through which I can all the more closely contemplate our Lord, adoring him not because of what he does for me or is for me, but simply because 'He *is*'. In pondering in my heart as Mary did, I realise that part of the calling is to be like Mary in a particular way – prepared to be so close to Jesus that it hurts.

Mary's surrender was not a reluctant compliance but a willing eagerness to say 'Yes' to the Father. This is what I still learnt, through all the spiritual growing pains: that we are simply to increase our receptivity of God. In the strivings, I always seemed to remark that no sooner was I resurrected than I was back on the cross. Now, with new vision, I see *all* of life as a privileged gift. No longer am I seeking to concentrate on the dramatic, exhaustive offerings but upon God alone, and upon discovering holiness in the ordinariness of daily living. The gift is in discovering and honouring each day, each moment, the Nazareth which is given to me; the Gethsemane which I may, at times, fleetingly pass through on the way to Calvary (be it my own, or that of a loved one whose suffering I may powerlessly be called upon to watch, as Mary did), and now the Resurrection . . . an abundance of life and joy, and laughter and trust . . . with frequent 'letters from home'.

LIVING THROUGH LOVE

Brian Grogan

Brian Grogan joined the Jesuits in 1954 and has worked in administration and in formation. At present he is completing a term as director of Jesuit novices near Ballymun in Dublin. To make the riches of Ignatian spirituality accessible to lay people, he has led numerous workshops and written extensively.

Out of turmoil and temporary insecurities, Brian discovers the love of God and the love of friends as 'the deepest reality' underpinning his life. He chose his title 'to convey both that I'm alive because I'm loved, and that I'm trying to live by love now, rather than from any other motivation'. This is a testimony of life-giving grace which moves a person from head to heart and from heart to spirit in a way which lets one enter more compassionately into the lives of others.

K.O'S.

21

As I write, my life is in turmoil: two good Jesuit companions are seriously ill with cancer; two other friends are moving away to missionary work, one to Nigeria, the other to Pakistan; I'm terminating a seven-year spell in formation work and facing a bewildering set of possibilities regarding my next assignment and its location. Nothing seems secure right now . . . except one thing: I *am* sure of love – of the love of friends and the love of God. I trust this love as the deepest reality underpinning my life. Hence the title I chose: it's meant to convey both that I'm alive because I'm loved, and that I'm trying to live by love now, rather than from any other motivation.

My present sense that well-established securities are fading echoes a parallel experience some seven years ago after a therapy session. I was on a long car journey and somewhere, as the miles slipped by, the words flashed into my mind: 'It's all been a great mistake!' What was a great mistake? A whole way of going about things – task-oriented anxious striving, meeting others' needs and ignoring my own, taking on too much and being over-responsible, rushing around and living in a state of underlying tension. As I continued on, it seemed that with each passing mile I was being liberated from a false way of being in the world. I also found myself wrestling with the question: 'Well, if it's all been a great mistake, if the maps I've been relying on are wrong, how do I proceed?' Then I found myself laughing: I checked in the mirror – yes, I *was* laughing. Only later in talking with a friend, did I come to see how graced an experience I'd been through. I'd been stripped of an illusion in a most delicate way that left me feeling, not depressed or ashamed, but at peace, even happy. I'd undergone a deft piece of surgery that left me not crippled but eager to take up life again, even if tentatively. I had also had an experience of divine humour: if I were laughing over what had happened, surely God was too!

Experiences such as the above don't come to me often: perhaps I'm not sensitive enough to them? Perhaps 'the voice of the Lord resounds' more often than I think? Occasionally I obey the advice of St Catherine of Siena that we should ask Jesus to reveal himself to us, since he has promised to do so (cf. John 14:21). To my surprise, this prayer always works, which makes me cautious about it! Two instances may be worth recording, since they link in with my theme. The first was during a phase when all seemed confused. I was going round and round on the question: 'What's life all about, anyway?' In an empty moment the answer came with luminous clarity: 'Life's all about God.' A few years later when feeling mad with a driver who cut in on me in heavy traffic, I sensed that I was being communicated with in a gentle yet serious way with the phrase, 'God's mood is loving, always'. Again I found myself smiling at the delicacy of the reproof. I was being loved in my particular mess; the shadow side of my life was being respected but also reshaped in a graced way. While I have little difficulty now in believing that God is deeply and irrevocably in love with everyone, I need reminders such as the above incidents offer, that God loves *me* in the same way. Put together, they read: 'Yes, you make plenty of mistakes, but I love you through them all. Try not to focus on anything less than God, that is, on anything less than love.' The voice resounds . . . and it is tinged with laughter.

When did I begin to notice that God's gracious love not only encompasses us all in some vague general way, but encircles me in all my particularity? I won't know the answer until the connectedness of all events is revealed at the end, but looking back I can see the touches of God's loving care in a secure childhood, steady parental concern, patient and self-sacrificing commitment to my good. These realities overrode the discordances of enduring marital tension at home. And while a few bombs fell in Dublin during the forties and rationing was severe, life for me as a child and teenager was safe. The love shown me at home was real, even if demonstrations of affection were strictly limited by Victorian guidelines. I can now see that God was busy about my good, while respecting the limits of local circumstances. I took it all for granted. I was being led by leading strings of love, but had little sense that it was God who was looking after me (cf. Hos. 11: 3–4), though of course I demanded of God whatever I wanted, and called it prayer.

Having decided early on that the world needed a lot of help if it were to be put to rights, joining the Jesuits was a relatively easy choice. That decision was preceded by a prolonged period of quiet attraction for God. I found joy in sneaking into the chapel beside our school and praying in front of the Blessed Sacrament. This experience was gift: I found it there, unsought. I often ignored it, yet it survived remarkably well along with the attraction of sports and a wholehearted if mindless allegiance to the Dublin football team. If grace is all about good relationships between persons both human and Divine, I was being well catered for at this time. As I write, it strikes me that the laconic Ignatian phrase, 'God wishes to give Godself to me, so far as God can', was being verified in those quiet times.

The long years of Jesuit formation were happy ones. I

was full of zeal, anxious to do well, and to get going in sorting out the human mess. Theology delighted me as I began to get to know more clearly what God is doing in the world. The private relationships which give each of the three divine persons limitless delight, and the mystery that they should want to share this delight with humankind, enthralled me. Again, this attraction and fascination was given: I found it in myself, unasked for and unmerited. As I write, I can see a link between what was missing in my little world at home, and what is intensely present in the relationships of the three divine persons. Perhaps the imperfect was the ground of my yearning for what was perfect in God?

My seven years studying theology were rich, and yet something was missing. Personal experience of the truths of faith was either ignored or treated with great reserve. I studied theology just after Vatican II. Thirty years later I find it sad that the new *Catholic Catechism* still bypasses the world of human experience. I now teach theology part-time, and I think of it as a mutual revelation, a dialogue between God and ourselves and I picture Christian life as a dance in which each partner respects and spontaneously adjusts to the other's initiatives. But in my student days head dominated over heart, and so it has come about that while we priests serve the people committed to us with total fidelity, the intimacy of relationship between God, ourselves and the Christian community seems often to elude our grasp. It's as if the party is in full swing, but we're the spectators at the window. It's a great blessing when God takes us by the hand and brings us inside.

For me the shift from head to heart began when, as a young priest, I began to listen to the stories of other people. There were those who seemed to be 'in with God' in a way that left me puzzled, embarrassed and fascinated. I wanted to have what they had: a sense of God as someone intensely personal and as deeply involved in all the details of their lives. There were others for whom life was falling apart: they came along to share their pain, and in hope of more help than I had to give, because their experience was not mine. They jolted me out of a complacency with my steady, predictable, well-arranged life. They made me wonder whether God is *really* good, and capable of dealing with the suffering and evil of the world. These questions are still with me, but the tragic stories I was hearing brought home to me that so much of what I had taken for granted in my own life was in fact the visible sign of the unique and special care of God. This brought me to a humbled sense of gratitude. Whatever those less fortunate than I might be able to say, I could truly acknowledge: 'God, you have been good to me, and I am grateful.'

In the early eighties a brief immersion in the Third World, first Somalia and then India, opened up to me worlds of shattering poverty and hopelessness. God seemed to have no ear for the cry of the poor: divine providence seemed absent, and the human predicament out of control. 'My child dies!' So said a Somali woman as she asked me for medication and searched my face for hope. And I had nothing to give. It is painful for me to admit that now. From my present perspective I know that in my total poverty God is present and active in ways of which I may know nothing. God lavishly fills human emptiness. Trustful prayer for that desperate woman would have been the loving response to her plea. More and more my prayer has become an intercession for a needy world. Its effectiveness is hidden from me, but will be revealed, I believe, at the end. The invisible presses in on the visible at every point, sustaining and transforming it, but naturally we can't see the process at work.

Two searing questions remained with me over the years from that time: 'Why do people have to suffer so much? And why is God so good to *me*?' Neither was answered, but God kept working steadily at the task of breaking down the walls around my heart. The suffering I endure in seeing the pain of others opened me up to people around me. I also endured considerable pain myself for some fifteen years with osteo-arthritis: two hip replacements have made me well again, but I know that what I suffered helped to make me more sensitive to others, though I didn't appreciate this at that time. Slow learner! I also became aware of a recurring pattern: that for as far back as I could remember, there was always someone in my life whom I found hard to love. The insight slowly came that these people were the instruments by which God was trying to stretch my love, and I the instrument to show to them what God's love is like.

From being task-centred I began to become more person-centred. I no longer felt that with enough energy and resources, the world could be brought to rights. Being-with others began to blend with being-for. Journeying-with became my favourite image: giving and receiving, sharing joys and sorrows, encouraging each other to keep moving and hoping. And in my forties came another breakthrough. I fell in love: defences crumbled, heart took over from head, vulnerability was respected, intimacy replaced aloofness. I came to know what it means 'to live through love' on both the human and the divine levels. Happily, through good and honest communication the inevitable tensions were resolved, so that human loving enhanced rather than rivalled divine loving. I was indeed brought inside into God's world of gracious love. I have been richly blessed with friends, God's chosen escorts of grace for me, and I in turn for them.

To the question, 'Why is God so good to me?' I now need no answer. God is just that sort: pure love acts with pure goodness, and God, who is such a good neighbour to me, invites me to 'go and do likewise' to others. No direct answer comes to the other question, 'Why do people have to suffer so much?', except the same invitation: 'Act with pure goodness towards others in the ways I open out for you. Walk with me and be open to being sent where I wish.' And so the story of grace in my life continues to unfold.

The mystery deepens, but is ever richer. My faith is stretched to breaking-point by evil, suffering and death. The dark side of the paschal mystery is very close, especially at present; if its brighter side now gleams fitfully rather than with the steady radiance which will come later, I still see it as the only parable that gives ultimate meaning to my life and the lives of all of us who play our brief roles in the drama of human history. I know I'm being changed while playing my role. I see others being changed too. I see less dimly what God is up to: how grace works undeterred and steadily through both the easy and the awkward people in my life, through the things I do and those that happen to me. The goal? To make me become love and so to ready me for eternal companionship with everyone, both human and divine, when the joy and laughter will be endless.

THE PRODIGAL MOTHER

Roisin Smyth

Roisin Smyth is married with four grown-up children and has taught in a kindergarten for the past twenty years. She is very active in parish prayer groups based on Light out of Darkness and has specialised in leading elderly people and the marginalised.

The real depth of this story is the incredible love of a mother who lets herself be turned upside-down, to distance herself from the 'problem', so as to see the truth of her own shortcomings. Her children had a vital role in this new experience of love – human and divine – which filled that home.

K.O'S.

I remember very vividly when my only daughter arrived home unexpectedly and, after supper, told me that she was pregnant. At first, I wondered what she could possibly be talking about. It was only when she burst out crying that I understood and was able to put my arms

29

around her and say, 'You are still our only daughter and this will be our grandchild.' We talked for a while and I took her hand in mine and, with the firm belief that all life comes from God, I said to her, 'Let us say a prayer for this new life.' (What the words of our prayer were, I cannot remember.)

We went to bed early. I just wanted to get under the blankets and blot it all out but that didn't happen. I twisted and turned but couldn't think straight. I knew I needed my God badly, but I couldn't pray. The words of a favourite hymn were all I could say:

You will show me the path of life and guide me to joy
    forever.
Keep me safe, my God. You, who are my only hope.
You alone will be my saving God.

This hymn was the only focus I had for the next three days as I struggled to function at my regular routine. Eating was a dreaded problem as I forced food down. On the third evening after this news, I went to a prayer meeting and gradually began to talk to God about it all. He brought me to the scene in the Old Testament where Abraham was asked to sacrifice his only son and Abraham was ready to obey. I realised that my daughter had been a gift to us for a short number of years but now God wanted her. In his hands he could do much with her, whereas I could do nothing. I was able to hand her over to him in faith and trust. It was like a mighty load being lifted off my heart. I could think straight again and eat without fear of choking.

Next day I was able to share this news with a praying friend – another easing of the burden. This friend became my 'Elizabeth' with whom I could find Jesus. The following day, 'Elizabeth' called with a lovely piece she had found, *The Sacrament of Letting Go*. It was the sacrament I most needed but I was still too shaken to begin to look at what I must 'let go'. A week later, at a reunion of a Light out of Darkness group, one member shared a prayer she had found, which started:

> Empty me of angry judgments, aching disappointments and anxious tryings and breathe into me something of quietness and calm confidence, so that the lion and lamb may lie down together in me and be led by a trust as straightforward as a little child.

It was surely for me. It named some of the hard knots I had managed to push down and keep well out of my thinking. I carried this prayer in my pocket. Very often it sat on the dashboard of my car as I beseeched God to do for me what I couldn't do for myself, to empty and fill me.

A few days later we were shattered by the news of the sudden death of a good family member. I hadn't shared our daughter's pregnancy with any members of the family yet, nor could I now with this added grief. I returned from the funeral outwardly seemingly intact, but I was just about holding together. An amount of post awaited me. One letter was from a member of our prayer group offering her sympathies and giving me this quotation:

> And I said to the man who stood at the gate of the year: 'Give me a light that I might tread safely into the unknown.' And he replied: '. . . put your hand

into the hand of God. That shall be for you better
than light and safer than a known way.'

Clinging to that strong hand I went to bed and slipped
into peaceful sleep. My God was taking care of us all,
my child and my grandchild.

Christmas was fast approaching but I found it harder
than usual to begin the preparations. Morning Prayer for
Advent in our Church was very important to me. 8th
December was especially significant with the liturgical
focus on Mary and what she had to face when she accepted
that special baby. I remembered my daughter telling me
that she was asked if she wanted to keep this baby. I was
so grateful to God that she wanted to say 'Yes'!'

Christmas brought family together and some difficulties for me. Her brothers were very supportive of their
sister, giving broad hints that my attitude would dictate
how neighbours and friends received the news. One night
as I tossed and turned, I came downstairs to coax sleep
with some hot chocolate. As I waited for the milk to boil I
opened the *Tablet*, seeking Jesus as usual. My astonished
gaze rested again on the words: '. . . put your hand into
the hand of God. That shall be for you better than light and
safer than a known way.' The quotation ended: 'So I
went forth, and finding the hand of God, trod gladly
into the night. And He led (me) towards the hills and
the breaking of dawn in the lone East.'

I was bowled over and truly elated. In faith, I knew his
hand was waiting and I felt enfolded. Happily I tripped
back to bed and to the gift of blessed sleep. Since then
I have spent many nightly hours being led peacefully
'to the breaking of dawn in the lone East' and gazing
at God's great love for each of us as he lies in a humble

manger. It is so hard take in. This little helpless baby –
totally dependent on humans – is God's Son. No clinging
here to his rights as the Son of the Creator of all, nor to
his divinity.

Against the backdrop of this scene, I began to see a
little of the real darkness which was causing me such
pain. I needed to be honest. I needed to dig deep and
let the root causes of my pain surface. My sons had
already pointed the way. God was using them to teach
me something. To what was I clinging? Was it pride in a
family tradition that did not accept, nor look favourably
on, unmarried mothers? Was it my reputation as a 'good'
mother that was damaged? I began to see that a good
bit of my concern had to do with me and my kingdom.
Such folly! Gradually, I have been enabled to let go of
much of this; I have been set free. But because it is so
ingrained in me, the marks reappear from time to time
and the struggle goes on. I realise that I must let go of
my pride, my human respect and my over-concern for
myself. I find now that energy that was spent on myself
is now extending to greater love and understanding of
my daughter. On reflection I can see more clearly that
my prayer must now extend to all who are experiencing
similar difficulties.

Because I am so frail, the darkness nevertheless began
to gather again. As always, I turned to Jesus. He led me to
meet his mother. Sitting with this most gentle of women, I
marvelled at her courage as she faced the consequences of
her 'Yes'. How did she do it? In prayer I seemed to hear her
say, 'All I had was my trust in God who loved me.' Yes, I
knew that was required of me too, but I felt so weak. I
confided in her my difficulty in sharing the news with
family, friends and neighbours. She pointed out to me

that when she received her baby, she was fortunate to have Elizabeth, a woman of great faith, in whom she could confide. Once again darkness began to lift as I praised and thanked God for his gift to me of a few 'Elizabeths'. I was not quite ready to let go; I still had to have a childish moan! I said, 'It is just a pity that my daughter wasn't married to the father before she received this baby.' And the answer came very clear: 'It would have been so much easier for me, had I been married to Joseph when I was asked to take my special baby. Remember God's ways are not my ways.' (I recalled that I had heard this from one of my 'Elizabeths' but had lost it in the darkness.) How patient almighty God is with me!

This year St Patrick's Day and Mother's Day coincided with the bonus of an extra day's holiday. All my children were coming home and I was busy. Trepidation and tension began to build up in me. I knew it was time for a quiet space with my Lord! It was time well spent. He made known to me that all that was required was a warm welcome. I am blessed with friends who care and who pray and who had promised to pray for a happy time for my family. I met my daughter at the airport clutching the 'hand' of Jesus which filled me with a quiet peace. My daughter was hugged with genuine warmth and love. The weekend was delightfully relaxed. As I sat at the table on the morning she was leaving, I felt a wonderful peace in being able to love my child as she is and not as I would like her to be. This was a mighty miracle. I thank God for all those friends who were praying for me and I value what it is to be part of the body of Christ. I know now, because I experienced it, that one is never alone. As my daughter hugged me she said how happy she was to come home. It was wonderful also that we were at peace as she left.

It was a moment of great freedom – being able to let her go. I knew that she was, as indeed I was, in 'safe hands'. I knew more fully also how God 'is showing me the path of life and guiding me to joy forever'. I am being led out of my darkness of expectations and pride into his wonderful light.

I know that the story and the struggle hasn't ended. Recently I was drawn to a tree with new, bright green shoots. On looking closer, I saw some old brown leaves still clinging to it. I am deeply aware of the 'old brown leaves' part of me too. They will be displaced I feel sure in time, when my pride and false expectations become humility and compassion for *all* God's people.

WALK IN THE LIGHT

Dan Joe O'Mahony

Dan Joe O'Mahony of Upton, Co. Cork, is a Capuchin friar and press officer for the Capuchin Order in Ireland. He has worked as chaplain to schools, colleges and institutes as well as with lay Franciscans and the Light out of Darkness ministry.

A true son of St Francis speaks in this testimony. Through it, respect and dignity are restored in some measure to today's 'lepers of society' in Coolmine Therapeutic Centre. The genuine love of Christ – which heals and unites both parties – is crystal clear; the prayer 'Bless them, Lord, who have so blessed me tonight' bursts from the heart of the priest who has celebrated the Eucharist with God's hurting sons; the conversation pieces, which appear like rich jewels, reveal the trust and love of the patients for their friend to whom they can reveal with minimum words their hurt and yearning for their own. Love is the bonding.

K.O'S.

36

'Amazing grace that saved a wretch like me . . . I once was lost but now I'm found . . .'

Saturday night in Coolmine is for me the most meaningful liturgy of each week. On that night, we, today's lepers of society and I, celebrate the Eucharist. How often I say to our young lay Franciscans – Brendan, Damian, and Ronan – who delight in preparing the music for us: 'But for the grace of God, there go I.' And each Saturday at the close of that Eucharist, at which Christ nourishes all of us – but me somehow most especially because he chooses his beloved needy ones to mirror God's own goodness to me, I say in my heart: 'Bless them Lord, who have so blessed me this night.'

Picture to yourself a group, aged about twenty-one or so, gathered in the upper room around the eucharistic table. They have been abused, damaged, jailed, ignored and forgotten for periods of time – hurt and hurting – and there you have the Coolmine Therapeutic Centre, Dublin 15.

Listen to their prayers, to their reaching out to those who listen, and you too will be healed of your blindness and darkness, as I am being healed. One prayer after the other, it touches, it pierces with laden tragedy, it moves one to tears:

'Let us pray for my mother, she's alone now . . .'
'I pray for my brothers out there on the street. God I ask you, get them in here for treatment . . .'
'Lord, I pray for the family here in Coolmine and for the girls up in Ashley . . .'

'I want to pray for my wife and kids . . .' and on it

goes, sincere, real and heavy with brokenness and sadness.

It is their pain, their vulnerability, their honesty that bring tears to my eyes so often. My broken brothers and sisters unashamedly bring their prayers to Jesus, trusting him, they who have so few to trust. And my former mask-wearing weighs heavy upon me, but they teach well in Coolmine!

As a Franciscan Capuchin, I now see – from my own experience – how Francis' encounter with a leper is a healing touchstone for all encounters. It renews our lives. It is there that we experience life as it really is for many. And it is in the middle of that forsaken life, full of rejection, that I learn to meet, to know and to love the *real Jesus*. My Coolmine friends have become instruments of salvation used for me by the mercy of Jesus. Masks have no meaning in the midst of this reality.

'Father, could you write out the words of the Our Father for me? Will you be up on Wednesday to give us the Ashes? Would you have more scapulars on you or beads? I promised a fella . . . Pray for me on Wednesday, I'm going for a test (HIV).'

Maybe this reaching out is as an excuse to communicate, maybe out of desperate loneliness – does it matter why? When you let yourself experience Jesus in these lonely, despised, hurting people, miracles happen within yourself. When I listen to my outcast friends singing their hearts out during the Mass, I recognise the special magic and power of music to soften hearts and lower barriers. The room becomes electrified with the love of the compassionate Christ, and in a strange way I feel that my heart, my face muscles have been touched and healed. Salvation happens in Coolmine – the Saviour I meet there is fully alive and his love overflows.

As a child in West Cork, my grandmother's picture of the good shepherd and the lost sheep left an indelible mark on me. Coolmine brings it all back to me. Despite the pain, there is in Coolmine a kind of quiet rejoicing at times. I think it is because the good shepherd helps his lost friends there to look for the one per cent of themselves that has been lost. When they find it, there is a surge, an uplift that somehow spreads to the remaining ninety-nine per cent of themselves. There grows a feeling that part of them – lost through no fault of their own perhaps – has been reclaimed, and this readies them for a healing. They reveal amazing courage and honesty in admitting who they are. They teach me. They reach out, in their way, in their language. I turn as I hear, 'Dan, how are you feeling tonight?' or more often, 'Dan, how is your space tonight?' And, unlike their free counterparts 'outside', they *want* to know; they listen and they care!

They reveal to me parts of myself that I have buried in my subconscious. They make me more aware, as I talk with them, of my own great lack of awareness – because I let myself become so busy! My latent anger comes to my awareness more easily in the open atmosphere of Coolmine than in my own monastery. They are wise somehow in our futile attempts at deception. They *see*. They have become prison-wise! They may not be familiar with the classical quote, 'There is no art to hide the mind's construction on the face', but they know and they do not judge.

The need for true humility on my part springs to my

awareness whenever I spend time with my Coolmine friends. My Franciscan awareness of the brotherhood and sisterhood of us all is more clearly challenged in Coolmine than anywhere else. They have their struggles, I have my own brand. They are not inferior to me or to others. In so many ways they are more caring and kind than I often am – and I have received so much help in life. I have social and family support, which many of them have not. I recognise changes in myself, necessary changes from attitudes that spring from power. We have the wherewithal to help, but it is so easy to use the old and fault-ridden way of the colonisers. And so I have become aware of not trying to change their lives, nor of getting trapped on the unhealthy treadmill of control or co-dependency. I have become aware of the insult to their dignity if I try to manipulate their choices to reflect mine; I try to stand with them, as they are, who they are, with their history, in their circumstances. Poverty has many forms, all of them difficult to accept, especially the poverty of being addicted and powerless as many of them can be. It is salutary for me to look at the poverty of my own creaturehood, at my personal sinfulness and my neglect of the grace of total dependence on God. I, who know I have nothing but my nothingness, yet also know that in having God, I have all. *Knowing* that, however, is not 'doing' it. What addiction prevents my doing that which will glorify God and help my brother?

Lost sheep cannot get back on their own feet when they roll over on their back. Sheep can wander out of fright or neglect, but tender, loving care draws a response from them. We are all lost sheep some of the time. Sheep can get knotted up in thorns. They become powerless to free themselves. They lie there, waiting for the rescuing hands of caring human beings. It is a privilege to take the initiative of love, of following Christ's selfless love, and going with him to help get lost sheep back on their feet. I rejoice that when I was lost, I was found. Gratefully now I am allowed the opportunity of helping those who hopefully in their turn will become wounded healers. My sin was that human respect was more precious to me than humbling truth, and only the truth sets free. I have missed too many golden opportunities of acting out of a living faith that recognised my brother as brother, my sister as sister, and my God as the only one who can save. Coolmine has released me enough that I desire to know my own darkness better. From the time I owned and claimed my real, frail self, who nevertheless ardently desires to seek and to follow God alone, I have revelled in walking in the light. I keep learning that when I let any twisted knots of personality be untied I can relax in the warm glow of peace and serenity that allows me to rest and sleep like a child of God, as Francis did. My Coolmine friends ensure that I keep the edge of my ardour sharp and clean!

The song 'Standing outside the Fire'[1] by Garth Brooks speaks to me, as it does to many in Coolmine:

> We call them cool,
> those hearts that have no scars to show,
> the ones that never do let go,
> and risk the tables being turned.
>
> We call them fools
> who chance the sorrow and the shame
> that comes from always getting burned.

[1] From the album *In Pieces* by Garth Brooks, Pearl Records, 1993.

But you got to be tough when consumed by desire
'Cause it's not enough just to stand outside the fire.

So, what will be our final prayer in Coolmine tonight, where God is saving on many levels, using various instruments? It has to be the one and only, their favourite and mine, 'Walk in the Light'. With such marvellous gusto, those words are sung and truly Heaven seems close and alight!

To love one another till the Saviour we meet,
Walk, walk in the light.
He lives today, He'll be your friend,
Walk, walk in the light.
Jesus did just what He said,
Walk, walk in the light.
He healed the sick and He raised the dead,
Walk, walk in the light.
Jesus died on Calvary,
Walk, walk in the light.

There is something deeply moving in the yearning and hope – born out of desperate need at times – that can resound in Coolmine, something authentic. They seem to stand naked before God and before humanity; and God, finding them in such straits, fulfils the words of Ezekiel (16:14): 'He clothes them with his own beauty.'

'Dan, before you go, can I have a "rap" with you? Dan, can I have a medal for my mother; is it blessed?' (It will lie close to the lad himself that night.) 'Dan, bring me a medal of Padre Pio next week.' One prepares to leave Coolmine; one is renewed, grateful, humbled, silent, praising, glorifying and thanking God. But there are lonely hearts still waiting: 'Dan, I believe Jesus is great. Yes, Dan, Jesus did just what he said. He is real for me now, real for real sinners. O God be merciful to me a sinner.'

And *I*, when I approach God, am I the Pharisee or the tax collector? Is my focus more on me and on my sins rather than trustingly on the love and mercy of God who loves so intimately his lost sheep?

He saved the lost like you and me
So let me lift my head,
Put back my shoulders and,
Walk, walk in the light,
With my hand in God's
And my arms on the shoulders of my brothers in
Coolmine.

FALLING IN LOVE AGAIN

Ivan Mann

*Ivan Mann originally trained as an engineer but then felt called
to the Anglican ministry. He re-trained in theology and was
ordained. He has been married twice – first to Jackie who died
in 1989 leaving him with four children. Now he is married to
Catherine, and they have two children. His ministry has been
spent in Suffolk, in both town and rural parishes.*

*Ivan was taking care of his wife who had motor neurone
disease. He was also responsible for the care of their young
children. It was at the lowest point of exhaustion and pain
that he found his God and fell in love with him again. 'I could
see my experience from his perspective for the first time and,
yes, I had known joy at the heart of the suffering.' The rest
of this touching testimony is about how God loved Ivan's
self-rejection into self-acceptance, and the role of prayer in
his new relationship with this God of love.*

K.O'S.

It must have been in the spring of 1987 that I sat down one afternoon to say Morning Prayer. I was looking after my wife who had motor neurone disease. The disease had developed after the birth of our fourth child so I was responsible too for the care of four children. I was tired beyond exhaustion. The routine of saying Morning Prayer whenever I could during the day was my lifeline. It kept me reading Scripture and, when words were beyond me, gave me words to say.

I said the office and then poured out exactly how I was feeling. One word summed it up – pain. As I came to the end of my complaining I looked at a picture on my desk. It was a wooden crucifix – the one that hangs outside the chapel at Fairacres convent in Oxford. As I looked, I heard myself say without thinking to Jesus, 'I love you'. The words came spontaneously, from the depth of my being. I knew that my love was merely a response to his for me. I had found God at the lowest point.

It was at that time in my life that one particular prayer was striking me forcibly – the prayer of Charles de Foucald. Part of the prayer moved me deeply, every time I prayed with it. 'I place my soul in your hands. I give it to you my God with all the love of my heart, because I love you.' In my journal I added, 'Whatever life does to us those words stand as true for me. However black the day, God's love for me and my love for him are the bedrock of faith. When all else is stripped away that love remains.' My wife died in 1989 and I returned to parish ministry a changed man. I had discovered that God was there even in the 'muck' of life. I had also discovered muck in my life which seemed impossible to handle. I knew that I could never be the same again and that God was calling me to a greater intimacy with him.

In October 1990 I went on an individually given retreat. I wanted to explore this intimacy. Before I went on retreat I had an image of how I was. I was a clenched fist holding myself in, like a prized coin. I knew that God wanted my hand relaxed and open – open to receive and to give, and I knew that only his love could achieve it. As the retreat went on there were many surprises and many challenges, not least the challenge to let go of my old images of God and allow the risen Lord to become real for me in a new way. I was to discover that when I think God has finished with me he has another gift waiting around the corner. So it was on this retreat – having been drawn into closer intimacy with Jesus, I found myself deep in conversation with him about the experience of looking after Jackie. I had been praying with John: 'that . . . which we have heard, which we have seen with our eyes, which we have looked at and our hands have touched – this we proclaim' (1 John 1:1). As I prayed, I found myself wrestling with God. 'What do you want of me – to proclaim my experience of you in suffering?' The answer was clear, 'Yes'. I wrestled further. 'Why then did you allow . . .? What was . . . ?' Again the answer was clear, 'I was with you.' And then the challenge: 'People need to know that I am with them in suffering.'

I found it hard to take in, and wrestled furiously. In the end all I could do was sit down and write of my experience. It took me the whole of the afternoon. As I came to the end I looked again to God. I could see my experience from his perspective for the first time and, yes, I had known joy at the heart of suffering. It was there that I had fallen in love with him.

As I went to the evening Eucharist these thoughts were

still gently overflowing in love. It amazed me then to listen to the preacher talk simply and strongly about joy at the heart of crucifixion. It was the confirmation that I needed. My evening prayer was full of adoration. I sat before a copy of the Rublev icon of the Trinity and having had my feet washed entered the intimacy of love which exists between the Father and the Son. As I approached I asked what I was to do. The answer was clear, 'Stay with us. Go for us.' All very gentle, very real.

A few months later I went on another type of course, a course in professional development. There I discovered what I should have known – that God can use any situation to speak to us. As my professional life was reviewed someone asked a question about why the experience of caring for a terminally ill wife had been so rich. I answered with a clarity and conviction which stunned me. 'Because I found God in the shit.' And then I realised that the call to use the experience was being affirmed again. I had been found by God. I had been drawn into his love. I needed somehow to tell others, to show others. But I had also learnt that the place of reality – God's and mine – is the place of prayer.

It was not long then before I began exploring prayer more deeply – through retreats and courses and daily prayer but then through the Ignatian Spiritual Exercises. The opportunity of praying through these Exercises was an invitation into new life. Quite simply they set me free.

As I prayed through Jesus' life I found my own life being exposed and treated with great love by this Jesus who had become my lover. He could be nothing less than gentle with me but in his gentleness was a firm reality. As I was placed with him in the presence of the Father, I found that not only was my experience of caring re-examined but almost every experience of my life. God turned out all the muck and all of it was used to reveal more of him, not only in my prayer but in my experience of life.

I came to a fresh understanding of myself and of God. Yet it was more than a fresh understanding. It became a new way of living. If God accepted me as I am and wanted to use me as I am, if he was calling me and sending me gently but clearly, then my life needed to be shaped by him. It needed to be lived to his praise and to his glory. Quite simply I was head over heels in love with him – and still am. There was nothing I wouldn't give to him. He had loved my self-rejection into self-acceptance. He had opened my hand – to receive and to give. Gradually I realised that he was sending people to me, people who needed someone who would listen to their pain, people who had themselves fallen in love with Jesus and needed someone who would understand. This has all been his doing and a great delight.

And all the time he has too been calling me to go further – to allow myself to be used in different ways, challenging ways. There have been periods of immense struggle – a sense sometimes that every ounce of me is being taken by him, but the love has been overwhelming and the joy complete. He never ceases to amaze me by his love. For the last ten months I have found myself praying again the prayer of Charles de Foucald. I have found now a different translation. It says all that I feel and fills me with desire.

My Father, I abandoned myself to you.
Do with me what you will.
Whatever you may do I thank you.

I am prepared for anything, I accept anything.
Provided your will is fulfilled in me and in all
creatures I ask for nothing more, my God.
I place my soul in your hands.
I give it to you, my God,
with all the love of my heart
because I love you.
And for me it is a necessity of love,
this gift of myself,
this placing of myself in your hands
without reserve
in boundless confidence
because you are my Father.

It should not surprise me then that God has been drawing me to listen attentively to his calling, nor that when I listen to others I see him sitting before me – see him in the gay person struggling for acceptance, in the mother rejected by her children, in the husband struggling to look after a terminally ill wife. It shouldn't surprise me, but it does. It seems such an enormous privilege and the greatest joy. It leaves me always with the knowledge that what I am able to offer others is simply the willingness to listen and to love because when I, several years ago, cried out in my pain, he was there – listening and loving.

And I love him so much.

HIS HAND ON MY LIFE

Sheila Wrigley

Sheila Wrigley is actively involved in the work of Maranatha and also in her local Methodist church. Married with two grown-up children and with grandchildren, she is an organiser of the Light out of Darkness ministry in Manchester and in Wales, and helps lead retreats in various parts of the country.

Sheila's testimony will bring hope and joy to many readers. It witnesses to God's powerful action of love which transformed a woman with a poor self-image since childhood into a Spirit-filled leader of groups who in their turn leave darkness behind and walk in the light of God's presence. She writes: 'The years that have followed have been exciting times of new discoveries about myself and about God, and of seeing other people's lives also transformed.' None of this leadership was 'of my choosing, nor have I ever wanted it'. Sheila depends totally on God.

K.O'S.

In 1989 an event happened which totally changed my life.

At that time I was married with two grown-up children and had been a Christian as long as I could remember. There was a desire in my heart for a deeper relationship with God, but I didn't know how to go about it.

Then I was invited to go on a retreat. From the very first day, Jesus, whom I had known all these years in my head, came alive in my heart. Sitting alone that first evening, I wept for many hours as I became overwhelmed with an experience of his love for me. Knowing each individual intimately, God knew that I needed a living experience of his love in my heart before he could bring about some of the changes he wanted to in my life. Only then would I be willing to be clay in the hands of the potter.

Not only was I willing but I was eager to let him show me the real me, the person I was beneath the masks, many of which I didn't even know were there. This he began to do with a tenderness and reverence which, instead of crushing me at each new revelation, gave me back my self-respect as I began to recognise that his love is truly unconditional.

Looking back I recognise that God had prepared me for this retreat, which was to be a life-changing experience, by placing within me a desire to deepen my relationship with him. This is not to discount all the previous years of my walk with God, when I received countless blessings.

That week was the beginning of changes which have affected every aspect of my life. Jesus became my friend and counsellor, as well as my Lord and Saviour. I found that in talking to him I could ask questions and receive answers, something which I had never experienced before. He opened up passages of Scripture for me; things which I didn't understand he explained, sometimes by giving me a very clear picture which was relevant to what was happening in my life.

As the retreat continued God showed me, through his word, areas of my life and childhood hurts which needed healing. As Jesus revealed his heart to me, his tenderness, compassion and unconditional love, I wept as I realised the paucity of my love for him. Without condemnation he showed me just how weak, self-centred and full of pride I was, and as I recognised and repented of these attitudes, he promised forgiveness and healing. I began to recognise that this vessel, made of clay, is his abiding place, that I am the temple of the Holy Spirit.

This was an awesome thought and one which I found difficult to comprehend. Since childhood I had had a very poor opinion of myself. My father died when I was seven and therefore I had no paternal affirmation. I only saw my mother during school holidays as I was in a boarding school from the age of seven until I was sixteen. I had quickly learnt to fend for myself but underneath there were hurts and rejection. An ingrained attitude became: I can't do it, others can do it better, but I can help them.

As I grew older this attitude of helping others formed the basis of my spiritual life. When I met and married a deeply committed Christian with a powerful ministry, I could only see that my mission in life was to make it as easy as possible for him to use the many gifts that God had given him. God, however, wanted something quite different and when I returned home from my week's retreat, all my husband could say to the retreat leaders was, 'What have you done to my wife?' We both knew that the changes which had taken place could only have been brought about by the power of God's Spirit.

A few days after my return, at a meeting of local Christians which my husband was leading, much to his surprise I asked if I could address those present. I was known by most of the people there as being a person who preferred to remain in the background, who said very little, and who could usually be found helping with the refreshments. Imagine their surprise, and my husband's too, when I spoke with confidence and authority, sharing with them the transformation I had experienced during the previous week. It was visible to them all and God's Spirit moved powerfully that evening in their hearts, as a result of which twenty-four people made the Light out of Darkness retreat at a later date, and most of these became leaders.

The years that have followed have been exciting times of new discoveries about myself and about God, and of seeing other people's lives also transformed. He has opened the way for me to become a living, fruitful part of his body. I know that I have a mission in leadership, although this is not of my choosing, nor have I ever wanted it. Each day I grow in him as I depend upon him to fulfil this ministry in me. This can only come about as I learn to let go of my own self-centredness and become totally dependent upon my God.

I recognise now that the conversion I experienced during that first retreat was just the beginning of a journey which is continuing and which is full of surprises. I am being taught by God to be still and this has become an important necessity in my life. It is in the stillness that I find his real presence and I am learning to take the awareness of his continuing presence into the busyness of life. That is a lesson I badly need to learn because when I am too busy I can become forgetful and unaware of other people's needs and focus on myself instead of on God.

It has been a privilege during these past few years to be part of a team leading retreats and witnessing the mighty power of God's Spirit in action. Those who come to the retreats, which are in contemplative silence, are from different traditions, religious and lay persons, and many have never been on a week's retreat before. In the silence they become bonded together in a unity with Christ and with each other which goes beyond anything they have ever experienced. The time of sharing in small groups which happens once each day is a rich time of testifying to the movements of the Holy Spirit in each of their lives. It is such a privilege to be part of this and to watch Christ's life growing in the retreatants. I find myself being taught by God, learning from what I see happening in others, and through this he is continuing his work of renewal in my own life.

In one such group, after prayer and discernment, the team had placed a lady with a Jewish tradition, who had become a Christian, together with a German lady. They were both strangers to us and we knew nothing of their backgrounds. When the time of sharing came and the retreatants introduced themselves to each other, the Jewish Christian was horrified to find herself in the same group as the German lady. She was full of prejudice and hatred of the Germans and was very angry with God, and probably with us, for putting her in this position. During the next few days I saw the barriers between them come tumbling down and during the final sharing at the end of the retreat, the two ladies embraced and wept as they gave testimony to the powerful action of God in each of their lives. As a result of their sharing, many people were touched by the Spirit, which continued after the retreat had ended as the German lady stood up in her church the following Sunday, which happened to be Remembrance Sunday, and gave testimony to what had happened. God was showing me that even in the seemingly small things, such as a decision to make a retreat, it is important to pray and discern his will. Every decision and choice that I make is important to him and he wants to be part of it. Moreover, I see how God's goodness spreads: a discerning choice; the openness of two ladies; their witness, and all of this coming full circle and flowing gratuitously over me and others.

On another occasion, a lady who was having difficulties in the retreat asked for prayer. In praying for the removal of any blockage which was preventing her from experiencing God's presence, it became apparent that she needed to forgive her mother who had disapproved of her marriage to a man from a different Christian tradition. Her mother showed no interest in their two children, sending them neither birthday nor Christmas cards. At first she was totally unable to forgive her mother but after prayer and asking for the help of God's Spirit, she finally forgave her. This set her free to make real progress in her relationship with the Lord during the remainder of the retreat. This was not the end of the story. Some weeks later she wrote to tell us that on arriving home and going to see her mother, she was amazed to find, for the first time, her children's photographs on the walls of her mother's room, and presents for her to take home to them. God was showing us in a very graphic way that forgiveness brings release and freedom, not only to the one who forgives, but also to the one who is forgiven. Incidents like the above have built up my faith and personal relationship with God. What I would have missed if I had not said 'yes' to the making of that first retreat! In fact fear had almost prevented my doing it. Here again is the positive result of a discerned choice.

I have discovered that every new day and every person I meet is a gift from God. Hardly a day goes by without my hearing of, or seeing at first hand, the power of God's Spirit bringing healing to people's lives. I do not know what the future holds, but I do know that he calls me to live in the present moment, and to allow him to live in me. I can only praise, glorify and thank my God who takes such care of each one of us.

THE NOWNESS OF NOW

Ben Mackay

*Ben Mackay entered the de la Salle Brothers noviciate in 1961
and subsequently taught in Southsea before moving to the
community of St William's home school in Yorkshire. He
eventually left the religious life and became head of St Swithun's
primary school in Southsea. He married Judith, teacher of
hearing-impaired children, and had three sons, the second of
whom died shortly after birth. In 1993 Judith was found to
have breast cancer and died in 1995. Ben still lives in Southsea
with his two sons.*

*Ben's description of the difficulties of a young boy growing
up will find many echoes in hearts of readers: trying to
meet impossible standards of being 'a good boy'; trying out
a religious vocation which was not God's way for him;
learning painfully to understand his humanity a little better;
longing to love and be loved. Eventually: 'I heard the voice
of God – unexpectedly – when I met and married Judith
. . . she was agnostic and searching.' Together they grew
and developed and love embraced all. Then Judith developed
cancer. That was when Ben discovered the centrality of the
nowness of now.*

K.O'S.

I don't remember hearing the voice of God as a child. I heard messages of concern about my soul, and teachings, texts and prayers I couldn't comprehend, having been told that they were good for me. One day I would understand them. They would arm me as a soldier of Christ. I was also aware of deep-down fears, longings and yearnings – and for what I did not even ask.

I have memories of joy – spring's prodigality, summer profusion, the grasp of my father's hand on a walk together, the immensity of the still, starlit skies on frosty winter's mornings. I recall anxiety, anger and bewilderment at the cost – financial, emotional, physical and material – of my parents' task of bringing up ten children. I think I was lost as a middle child. I was moved, aching and longing for something else, something lost or out of reach.

I couldn't hear the voice of God in my learnings. The catechism answers, to questions I had not asked, were important but sterile. God was the docile boy Jesus imprisoned in the tabernacle – did he struggle to get out? God was also the angry judge of the Last Day. I knew I was unworthy, not a 'good boy'. I'd be dragged hellwards like the lost souls of Michelangelo's fresco. I couldn't hear God in the confusion of adolescent attempts to overcome the failure of the 11 plus, in trying to come first in class and getting good exam results, in fears about purity and the damned sixth and ninth commandments (rehearsed with blushing regularity), in questions about the goodness or otherwise of friendships – with either sex.

I wasn't sure that I liked God, even as I tried to love God. I wanted to get close to God. I did not feel that God could possibly want to get close to me.

I thought I heard the voice of God in a vocation to the religious life as a teaching Brother, in the admonitions to be 'good', to follow the 'counsels of perfection'. So I began to walk a path that was diverted from childhood's incomprehensible longings, from learning to love, recognise and hold myself, my feelings, my turmoils. The experience was alienating as I prayed that I would be (in ascending order of importance) a good person, a better Christian, a righteous Catholic and an excellent Brother. I learned to pacify and suppress inner angers, to work dutifully at serving others, to ignore the promptings of groin, head and therefore heart. I grew strong-shelled, like the lobster. I liked the admiration and security that seemed to go with it. But within, I was crying, confused and hurting, afraid to venture inwardly and therefore unable to risk beyond myself. I could not imagine that God was in the situation, calling me through it.

I listened for the voice of God and dared to believe it was in my choice to work with disturbed, delinquent boys. Initially I identified unwittingly with those whom I'd come to help. In successive moments of insight, painful in the coming, I owned my angry disturbance rooted in childhood. I realised I admired the reckless promiscuity of a youngster with whom I was close. It represented, perhaps naively, individuality, a breaking out from restrictions, a seeking for intimacy. I became intensely frightened and my shell began to crack open. I begged to hear God as I seemed to fragment, and I was gifted with the awareness that I was indeed loved through the concern, care and affection of some of the boys, my family and my community. I began to believe that I was lovable and capable of genuine loving. I grew, I became more trusting of my anxious heart, and eventually, even though I had earlier sought relief from tension by taking final vows, the decision to leave the Order came bubbling up from within with an unexpected serenity and conviction that I was really beginning to experience vocation.

I felt I heard the voice of God calling me in the decision to work in a Plymouth dockyard school, where I was enabled to trust my growth – away from my family and former community. By now, my much-loved parents had died. In long, lone walks on Dartmoor I touched more of the irreconcilable feelings of childhood. I struggled with and broke the image of my elders, which had been based on naive expectations born of infantile innocence. I felt further waves of frustration at being emotionally stuck in the past, anger at the messiness of childhood that seemed now to be present, and I was bursting to hold and be held. Paradoxically, the more I explored this, and made it the matter of my prayer, the more I grew up. God was in the painful experience of living alone, lonely at first and then in gentler solitude in which I grew to be more self-tolerant. I still struggled with God in my mind. I had yet to struggle truly with God in my heart.

I heard the voice of God – unexpectedly – when I met and married Judith. Her family were atheistic, she was agnostic and searching. I represented someone who had apparent answers. I was initially confused that she could possibly love me. After all, I was only recently learning to love myself. Yet in her loving I grew further, as we explored and experienced trust of self in each other – by no means easy, sometimes turbulent, invariably exciting. The voice of God was in the bonding and in the awareness that we were also separate.

God was surely in the birth of our three sons and the death after three days of our middle boy. How curious, now, that the middle one died. In the mixture of feelings at their births, of letting go of aspects of our former selves, of renegotiating life together, of confronting joy and the working out of earlier questions of nurture, holding and gradual separation there were metaphors for my struggling relationship with God. Through all this Judith sought baptism and we were truly together in searching for authentic faith.

I heard the voice of God calling in the diagnosis of Judith's cancer, in the intention to accompany her 'every millimetre of the way' through her dire double mastectomy, her chemotherapy and beyond. In the anxious weeks before diagnosis, I knew that my trust in God was on the line. In heaviness of heart, 'Why?' was counterbalanced by 'Why not?' There followed months of anguish, loneliness even, as we struggled to sustain ourselves and our two boys. We were accompanied by a vast praying army, loving us and hoping for us when we hardly dare hope. When the cancer matastasised Judith wanted a miracle. She begged me to believe, no, promise her, that one would be given. I heard the voice of God calling me not to write the script for the future – as ever, that was full of projected illusions. God called me not to dwell in the past; there was no refuge there, only present healing of anything unresolved from it. God called me to be truly present to myself, my own tears, fears and need to trust, because only then could I truly accompany my love. I explored my feelings, wrote them out into the open, talked about them to those who dared to ask, to listen and to hold. I confronted my fears of living and dying, my despair, my atheism, my longings for Judith, my boys and myself.

God called me to the abandonment of my fragile hopes, because only in this could I live in the nowness of now. They held conditions and God wanted the surrender of my cluttered head, heart and will in fullest trust. The pain of impending and apparent loss pointed to harboured illusions of the mind which were gradually put aside. I was moved to tears when Judith said she was 'willing to be made willing' to surrender all into God's keeping. In this were the beginnings of a healing far greater than the miracle cure – the healing of her heart.

God spoke in her courage as she was enabled to abandon her futile treatment. God spoke with tenderness as God drew her into an experience of gentle questioning through to fuller living of each moment into her dying into joy. It pained me deeply to walk with her, leading our boys too, into the laying before God of all our stripped-down selves. Early one morning before she died I heard God call when she murmured, 'No clothes, Ben', and we held each other in loving farewell. And I heard God as we held her and encouraged her to go with our love into the joy of God beyond death.

Now I hear God's voice very gently. God calls me to live each successive moment in God's company, to know that I am held, loved and able to love. God's voice reminds me that God holds my befuddled head and invites me to hand over all those tensions it entertains. God has my heart – indeed, I discovered that God always had it – as I pray that it be ever open. God has my will, not in despair, but in trust. I know I have been blessed, that God was, is and always will be with me. At heart, I know that God is with me in the stillness within. I used to believe in God. Now I believe God!

FAITH

All things spiritual are rooted for us humans in our humanity. What is visible leads us to the invisible. What is nearest to us – our human experience – leads us more easily into the divine.

Our growth in faith is greatly facilitated therefore by a felicitous human experience of trust. Too often our human experience of trust is betrayed but the fidelity of God never wavers. We must sometimes take a leap in the dark, put our hand trustingly – in faith – into a hand that does not grasp reassuringly; but that trusting in the dark and the unseen is when real trust is sown and faith begins to flourish. It takes courage; it also is supported and motivated by love and it blossoms into hope.

It is an interesting fact that in our contributions, the largest number focus essentially on faith; this faith to which we all aspire is a 'living faith'. It is faith in a person, who never leaves us alone, who empowers us with the strength of his own life, who continually overshadows us with love so that we breathe in hope.

TRUST IN GOD

Eilish Health

Eilish Health joined the Civil Service in London in 1961. She is now a bereavement officer with her local health authority and assistant chaplain in her local hospital. She is married with three children and a grandchild. She is a Catholic utterly committed to working with those of all denominations and, in the 1980s, became involved with lay spirituality and with Light out of Darkness. She has been trained in the Spiritual Exercises of St Ignatius and leads retreats and weeks of guided prayer.

Eilish, journeying as a child of ten caring for three younger sisters, knew there was no one to turn to but God. This she did in perfect trust. He did not fail her then or ever since. The wholehearted trusting of all her life, in little things as in the more important, is what has filled this writer's relationship with God with utter simplicity and transparency.

K.O'S.

I was ten years old. I had just seen my mother driven

away in a big blue ambulance, and I stood in the kitchen with my three younger sisters and said, 'Don't worry, everything will be alright.' A neighbour had come in to stay with us until my father could get home, and I felt very much alone. This was the first time I remember being aware that I had no one to turn to but God, so in my childlike way, I told him how I was feeling, and I could feel him put his arms around me and say, 'It's all right, trust me, I'm looking after you.'

As I look back on my life to that first conscious memory, I can see that the pattern that probably began when I was very young has continued. I grew into adulthood, marriage and motherhood, middle age and becoming a grandma, and always God has invited and drawn me to trust in his love and faithfulness. I can see a parallel between the way the God of the Old Testament related to the Israelites – with love and patience, with strength and power, with tenderness and compassion, always faithful and always there – and the way he relates to me. He has always been there, he has been there before me, and he invites me to trust him, and to say 'yes' to his gentle leading.

> Do not take fright, do not be afraid of them. Yahweh your God goes in front of you and will be fighting on your side as you saw him fight for you in Egypt. In the wilderness too, you saw him: how Yahweh carried you, as a man carries his child, all along the road you travelled on the way to this place.
>
> (Deut. 2:29–32)

My childhood was fairly nomadic, my father worked in the building trade and when one job was finished we moved to where another one started. I remember change and uncertainty, moving from one area to another, moving from one school to another, and having no adult to share with, so I seemed to talk to God continuously about my feelings of anxiety and fear. I learnt what it felt like to be powerless, and to have no one to share that with; and, in a way that I know nothing about, I came to believe that he was always there and always understood.

And so I grew into adulthood and left Ireland at eighteen for London. I had a job and accommodation, and I arrived at Euston station one late afternoon in September 1961. I can remember standing in what appeared to me to be an enormous and busy place. I was totally paralysed by the noise, the movement and the rush of people who all seemed to know exactly where they were going – all except me. And again I heard that familiar voice: 'It is all right, trust me.'

I had always enjoyed going to church, in being part of a community, and finding God in the beauty of the Mass. Now, a stranger in England, every time I went into a church the tears flowed. I was homesick. Being in a church, hearing the familiar words in a strange place, and feeling so alone made the homesickness more acute. So I stopped going to church. Foolishly I tried to run away from the pain, and to run away from God. But he did not run away from me nor let me slip away from him. Gradually I discovered that he was faithfully waiting beside me in my pain and tears, and that I was invited to find him there, where I was, however I was. So, I went back to church and cried my way through it all, aware that he was there, even though I did not feel or experience him as I used to do. But I found him in a new way, a way that was not comfortable and comforting, but was struggle and uncertainty, and yet it was God.

Teilhard de Chardin puts into words the way it felt: 'Only God could say what this new spirit gradually forming within you will be. Give our Lord the benefit of believing that his hand is leading you, and accept the anxiety of feeling yourself in suspense and incomplete.'

Life continued. I married, had three children, and on one level was happy and content. But there was always a ceaseless searching, a looking, a feeling that there was something, someone more. Then one day I heard someone speak about a God who was as much a part of everyday life as he was a part of prayer and church life – and I was bowled over. I felt, rather than saw, something of what she spoke of, and I can remember saying to her, 'I don't know what you are talking about, but you have a vision and I want some of it.' I did not know then, as I do now, that the Spirit of God moved in that desire which he had placed within me.

It was as if I heard his voice again, but there was a difference. The struggle and uncertainty I had experienced during my early days in England had somehow resulted in my growing up, in a maturing, and a growing into this new God, this new relationship. His voice now called in a different way: 'Come, find and discover. I travel with you always.'

And so began a most wondrous part of my journey with God – I had found a human being who really wanted to share her own journey, and in so doing help others along on their way to God. I learned about a God who was an intrinsic part of every aspect of my life, who loved me unconditionally, steadfastly, and was always drawing me into a deeper, closer relationship with him. I learnt about prayer and Scripture, about being more aware of what was happening within me and around me; and I learnt about the importance of reflecting on all that happened, both in my prayer and in my life, so that I could find God in it all. What a joy-filled adventure! I can vividly remember walking up the road in which I lived. The sun was shining, it was the same road, the same trees, the same pavement; everything was the same but everything was different because he was in it. And since then, not only the fact of his presence but the quality of his presence is a joy, a delight, a reason to praise and glorify him for his fidelity and care.

Some of my friends noticed that something in me had changed, and I shared a little about the treasure I had found. I can remember, a few of us wrote a piece for our church bulletin entitled 'Do you want to know the God who knows you?' A large group of people had a thirst for that 'something more'. They came to a meeting, and so began another cycle within the pattern of my life.

Through prayer, discernment and spiritual direction I began to see that God was inviting me to share with others what I had found. I had no degrees in theology, no certificates or qualifications in leading or in training others. What I had and still have is my unswerving faith in a God who has always been with me, always faithful. He has never left me alone or uncared for; never once has he let me down. So with the help and encouragement of friends and family I began to learn how to lead groups and retreats. I was eventually trained in spiritual direction and in the Exercises of St Ignatius, and this proved to be a time of great joy and enormous challenge. Growing, however, is often very painful, for having to let go of the familiar means change and a certain insecurity. I frequently felt as if everything I had ever known was taken away and that I was left naked and completely powerless. Yet, through all that time, when often I felt that this was all too much, when I felt like giving up, I would again be aware somehow that I could never really leave him, whose voice in the depths of my being kept saying without words: 'Trust me; just trust me – all is well.' I knew I could trust him in that moment, not tomorrow nor next year, but now. I could manage 'the now'; and in doing so peace took firm hold of me.

And that has been the pattern all through the years. The joy, delight, and privilege of being allowed to share with others some of my own journey, and of being given the gift to hear their story and to travel along with them, is a wonderful presence of God in my life. I hear his 'Trust me' not only in my own life, but in the lives of so many others who struggle to find him. In the changes and uncertainties of our lives many of us are invited to step out in faith, with no knowledge of what the future holds, and no guarantee of anything, except that deep-down feeling of trust that he is there before us. I finish with some words written by a friend who heard the invitation and responded wholeheartedly with his 'Yes':

All I am is 'Yes' to God.
I offer back to him my total self – the gift which
    he made
the gift which took all of his delight.
I give my 'Yes' to him in total trust, his faithfulness
    surrounding me
embracing, holding fast.

70

The 'Yes' is his – the all embracing arms and heart
delighting in the echoed 'Yes' – that is, in fact, no more
    than love,
my love, reaching for the Father's hand and heart.

THE LORD OF THE HARVEST

Ben Moran

Benedict Moran was ordained in 1968. He has ministered in the new town of Tallaght and in Waterford, and is now prior and director of St Dominic's Retreat House in Cork where he combines administration with retreat ministry and spiritual direction.

The Irish humour that graces this article serves to highlight the gentle depth of spirituality that rises easily from the heart of the writer and touches the reader. This is a most delicate description of the essence of a Light out of Darkness retreat.

K.O'S.

It is Thursday 20th July 1995. At long last a heatwave! People in Ireland have spent the last number of years looking forward to a summer of sunshine – just like we had in the good old days! The community and staff at St Dominic's Retreat House in Cork are busily preparing for the next retreat, called Light out of Darkness. In spite of the beautiful weather and the grounds of St Dominic's reflecting back the glory of God, it hasn't been a good summer for numbers attending retreats so far. Already one has had to be cancelled. And bookings for Light out of Darkness have slowly reached the fifteen mark. Another two or three would be necessary to make it viable.

The prior is wanted on the 'phone! 'Hello, Father – Tom here from the Isle of Wight. Would it be possible for my girl friend, Sara Jane, and myself to come as guests and stay for a few days?' I explain that it was not customary during the retreat season. And, then, inspired as it were by the Holy Spirit, I suggest, 'What about doing the Light out of Darkness retreat?' Tom is somewhat taken aback. 'What is that?' And being a bit smart I reply, 'Have you two hours and the money for this trunk call?' I give a short explanation but suggest that, if he is really interested, he should discuss the matter with his girl friend and perhaps call Mary O'Sullivan, an experienced leader of the retreat, for further clarification.

What a surprise and a delight on Sunday evening when the retreatants assemble to find Tom and Sara Jane in their midst. That to me was the first sign from God that this retreat was to be especially graced. God was gathering in his people: 'from age to age you gather a people to yourself.'

Many other signs quickly followed. The group was small in number, twenty including the three leaders, and it gelled beautifully. The composition was balanced and representative of differing ages, vocations, nationalities, denominations and varying gifts.

At the time of the faith-sharing it was apparent that many people had received the grace to touch into the darkness of their pain and to share with others in an atmosphere of faith. Mary, the leader, was a young economist, accustomed to studying the various market forces that determine the gross national product. When it came to the spiritual life she discovered a new law at work: 'My grace is enough for you: my power is at its best in weakness.' Echoes of St Paul could be heard ringing through her sharing: 'I shall be very happy to make my weaknesses my special boast so that the power of Christ may stay over me . . . for it is when I am weak that I am strong' (2 Cor. 12:9–10).

The sensitivity and compassion that was exhibited throughout the faith-sharing said to me that I was privileged to be standing on this holy ground and that God was indeed in this place.

The start to the retreat was difficult for some people. The amount of silence provided in the timetable was a strange experience for ears accustomed to a daily barrage of sounds. And the transition proved difficult. However, the caring support and the gentle atmosphere allowed the truth of the psalm to dawn gradually: 'Be still and know that I am God' (Ps. 46:11).

The Eucharist each day for me was the high point. In the chapel of St Dominic's the celebrant at Mass can look beyond the congregation to the surrounding fields and further on down the river Lee and Lough Mahon. The fields, in that warm and sunny July, were heavy with golden corn ripe for the harvest. I wondered to myself which group of retreatants this year would be blessed to witness the harvesting of such a beautiful crop of barley.

As we prayed at the offering of the gifts each day –

Blessed are you, Lord, God of all creation. Through

> your goodness we have this bread to offer, which
> earth has given and human hands have made. It
> will become for us the bread of life –

there was a sense that God was at work among these
beautiful people, lifting them up and building them into
the body of Christ.

Sometimes when saying Mass a priest can feel – rightly
or wrongly – that as presiding celebrant one is carrying
and leading and taking all the initiative. And soon he
becomes a functionary. It is a draining experience and
can happen to all priests at some time. Not so here. It
soon became evident that God had shared many gifts of
praise and intercession with this group, and that these
gifts were being returned to the Lord in the best way
possible. And as the Lord nourished his pilgrim people
at the eucharistic table this priest felt that he was on the
same journey from darkness to light and that he too was
being fed.

And, yes, it did happen! During the contemplative
silence on the Thursday I thought I noticed a slight
distraction coming from the great outdoors. Could it
be? And, yes, it was! The harvesting had begun. The
sun shone gaily throughout that long day as the harvest
was won: 'those who are sowing in tears will sing when
they reap' (Ps. 126:5). Our tears were being turned into
gladness. Our darkness to light.

FROM THE HEAD TO THE HEART

Mary McCaughey

Mary McCaughey is a student from Dublin. She has completed a degree in business studies and a diploma in theology, and now intends to study for a diploma in education in order to teach religion in secondary schools.

Mary's testimony highlights the problems besetting many young people today: the values of society inculcate an obsessive urge to climb to the top with, at most, a cursory glance at God. As a high achiever, Mary experienced emptiness of heart; life had little purpose and no real meaning. God however was reading the desires of her heart. A friend pointed the way which gave meaning to her life – prayer; the Spirit was moving in Mary, though she remained unaware at first. Finally through a group of young people, who thirsted for something better as she did, Mary came to know her real self and consequently the real Jesus. Her exciting journey of faith in Jesus continues as she recognises the importance of a group – the body of Christ.

K.O'S.

I am a twenty-three-year old student from Dublin. I suppose I have always been what psychologists term a 'high achiever'.

When I was in secondary school, I was the quietest and shyest person in my class and would never give an opinion or speak out loud if I could possibly avoid it. I was quite bright and hardworking and especially enjoyed languages and art. Besides English literature, which touched on some of the 'great questions' in life, and part of our religion course, I found that there was nothing in the curriculum which aims to encourage any sense of a person's self-worth, over and above how they performed in school subjects. And so I pushed myself hard to stand for something and be of worth to society by being 'intelligent'. I did think of going to art college, but my sense of responsibility and sensibility overruled any sense of the poetic inside me.

So I chose at the age of seventeen to begin a degree in business studies at Trinity College, Dublin. The college environment was exciting and new to me and I was eager to question the meaning of life and have 'great' philosophical discussions with students from all over the country! However I was soon to be disillusioned. Most of the students were either serious accountants who simply 'got on with their work' and saw themselves as shaping their own destiny or sociologists and political scientists who tended to be of the bohemian, hippy variety. From time to time I swayed between both groups trying hard to find my own sense of identity. I didn't even find my studies very fulfilling, but I pushed myself and for the last two years of college my life seemed to revolve around the library of Trinity College. I knew that if I didn't work, and if I stopped to consider the meaning of life, I would be tempted to drop out of society altogether. My course of study seemed so meaningless and irrelevant to the *real* questions in my life.

When I reached third year, I met Anne Marie. We got on well. She seemed quite serious and had a sense of purpose about her life which appealed to me. We began talking about friends, work, careers, purpose and . . . God. I soon learned that it was God who gave her this strong sense of purpose in life. Gradually Anne Marie encouraged me to pray. At first I could not talk easily to God at all. I would just ask him to bless everyone in my family, bless my work and help me through college. Beyond that, I felt what was the point; life had taught me that the rest was up to me. Anne Marie gave me books that began to get me thinking about living life as a true Christian and 'being holy' in the world. For me, the idea of 'being holy' did not ring true with 'being in the world'. I couldn't see any connection between all of the things I enjoyed (like dancing and friendships) and didn't enjoy (like cramming for exams) and God. I still preferred to try to sort things out 'by myself'.

From the age of thirteen I used to keep a diary. It varied from accounts of meals and clothes to reflections on friends and long descriptions of boys I admired and 'intensely loved' from a distance! In college these notebooks revealed more of my restlessness and most of the time I simply wrote furiously and angrily about how much I hated business studies and how unfulfilled I felt. My emotions had to be repressed in my day to day living, so it was my diary that contained how I really felt. I told Anne Marie that for me this was the same as talking to God and I know now that indeed God was with me and cherished the outpourings in my diary.

A Master's course in equality studies was my first attempt at doing something more fulfilling. And it was! I enjoyed discussing all the injustices in society which prevented people from leading fully human lives. We researched and debated women's oppression, and inequalities between the rich and the poor countries and in our own society. I was fired up to solve all the world's problems and ready to go to the third world as a lay missionary. But where was God in all this? Anne Marie had left Ireland and my image of God was too vague to satisfy what I know now was a deep inner search and need for truth. In fact I was soon to realise that I didn't know him at all. My image of God was like my image of society, as something that shapes us to conform to the image of the 'perfect citizen'. While I tried to impose on myself a time for prayer and for spiritual reading as Anne Marie had suggested, I seemed to do it more out of a sense of duty than out of any desire to love God. I wanted to rebel against this way of knowing God, yet I didn't know any other. I yearned desperately to come to know better the 'kind and gentle Jesus' whom I remembered from my childhood.

That year I spent a week on holiday and brought no books except my Bible. Why? I do not know. I was moved strongly to do so. I know now that the Spirit of God led me to do that in order that my mind be clear to listen to how he was going to speak to me. Looking back now, I see how God must have rejoiced when I began to admit how I didn't know him! I began to read St Paul's letters. In fact I could not put them down. Paul spoke so much about freedom and the Holy Spirit. The truth will set you free! Free, free, free. I reflected much on this. I knew at heart that I was really afraid of freedom. I did not know who I was and yet I knew that for true freedom I had first to know myself. The desire for a real personal relationship with Jesus began to move deeply within me. St Paul had alerted me to the shape of my life. I prayed to Jesus to help me. It was the first heartfelt prayer I had ever made. I feel this was a beginning towards something that drew me.

I had won a scholarship to do a Ph.D. in business studies which involved my lecturing and giving tutorials to people of my own age group. Everyone was thrilled for me. I had finally made it. But my heart said a strong and clear 'No!' Yet even at this stage I was not strong enough to follow my heart.

At the same time, I started a human spiritual growth programme called Light out of Darkness. This changed my life. A young Capuchin Brother helped lead my group. I was impressed by his gentleness, patience and reverence when we called upon the Holy Spirit. We experienced trust in one another which led to trust in God and faith in how he was speaking to us. We discovered how necessary it was to become real, open and genuine, letting go of all our masks and make-believe. We learnt to discover what our frailties and weaknesses were and to see for ourselves how this was affecting who we were and how we were living. We shared these experiences in trust in the group, and through this we grew. For me it was similar to the way I shared my experiences in my diary, only now I knew to whom I was writing! God became real in proportion to our own awareness of what was happening in our personal experience, and that opened the way to knowing him, trusting him and loving him. I was no longer lost; I was now following the path of Jesus as a Christian and I was not alone. God and his people were with me! I could now *experience* Psalm 139, not just read it as theory.

Gradually Jesus became a dear friend: he was real. It meant I had to give him time, attention, honest talking and listening, just as with a human friend. But I learned to enjoy it and, out of this, intimacy began growing between us. It was such a gradual, normal growth and I learned that this was the freedom I was yearning for: the freedom to live by his Spirit not only when I was alone with him but at all times. It became instinctive for me to pause, to be with him present in my heart, and to tell him about what was troubling and amazing me. Through his Holy Spirit moving me, I became quite sensitive to the way I behaved. I soon recognised when I was behaving for the benefit of others and not being true to my faithful and loving friend. He didn't get impatient with me but kept on loving me. How do I know? I know because when I gave him quiet time and was honest, I can't tell you the kind of *peace* that filled me. He was glad that I was home with him again. Sometimes I would rest quietly in his love and learn to trust him more.

I was no longer forcing Christian living on anyone. It all came so naturally: God is Love. I had the dearest friend who loved and affirmed me despite all that I did that was weak. Now I knew the good news I had to carry to others. I had to become the good news myself, the peace and joy and love and the other gifts of the Holy Spirit we read about in Galatians (5: 22–5).

One evening, I stopped off in a church. A group was singing the hymn 'Be not afraid'. I knew it well, but this time I heard it differently. Jesus was speaking directly to my heart. I began to cry, I felt so loved. I felt such relief. My life was all in his hands and he was going to look after everything. But I knew I had to remain close to him.

Soon afterwards I was led to give up my Ph.D. course. I prayed and reflected deeply, and knew that God was calling me to be 'my real self', the person I was trying so desperately to repress out of fear of 'standing out in the world'. Gradually Jesus led me into various forms of voluntary work in my parish with young people. I helped out in retreats and youth clubs and used talents that I didn't know I had. God showed me that I had a capacity for listening and an empathy for young people because I understood the deep pains of their search. Everyone of us is craving for this sense of unconditional love and acceptance and we search in all sorts of false ways to find it. We, as young people, search passionately for the truth because without truth we have no path to follow and no meaning in our lives. I know now that Jesus truly is the way and the truth and the life, but I have yet to learn to live that deeply.

I have become close friends with two people who have suffered mental illness and with another person who is addicted to drugs. Every day for them is a struggle – often against themselves. My image of the gentleness and faithfulness of God is constantly expanding and broadening through knowing these people. I praise and thank God for all that he has given me, all the opportunities to grow and develop. Above all, I value now the true gift – the gift of himself. Without the real knowledge of his love, my life would have continued empty and meaningless. All the striving in the world would have only isolated me further from him, and being isolated from him would mean being isolated from myself.

For me, learning to live with each moment just as it is, despite it not going according to my plan or perhaps being filled with interruptions from others, is God's way of showing me that he is in firm control of my life. As I gradually come to allow this to be the norm, I relax and I am filled with his peace. Sometimes I am tempted to feel that this is crazy, out of control, but then I laugh when I see how perfectly and lovingly he looks after me. 'Look at the birds of the air. They neither toil nor spin and see how perfectly my Father looks after them!'

Where it all leads I don't know, but I do know 'him whom my soul loves'. I have now the opportunity of being trained as a teacher, and at the moment this is my greatest desire: to bring God with me into the classroom, to teach young people to value themselves as persons loved unconditionally by God, to encourage them to love what is beautiful and to discover for themselves, in little ways, the need to choose to discipline their own waywardness in order to search in the right place for love and truth. It will not be easy but I trust that God will give me his strength and patience! He will also help me to use my own experience so that others can understand the importance of theirs and of personal responsibility. This brings all of us to continuing maturity – as Jesus, my teacher, has taught me and continues to teach me.

FINDING THE LORD IN POWERLESSNESS

John McGrath

John McGrath was born in Co. Clare. He has ministered in parishes in east London and Essex and is now parish priest of Our Lady of Lourdes, Leigh-on-Sea.

This straightforward testimony of the writer's experience of powerlessness is pertinent to the problems of today. He emphasises the reality of sin and what it is and the certainty of God's forgiveness and care. The positive side of the proper use of power is treated in a manner that points the way forward to a new growth. The grace of a living faith is clearly exemplified.

K.O'S.

Many people nowadays feel powerless. They experience this especially in efforts to change other people, rather than beginning with themselves. Twenty years ago, as a rather idealistic but naive young priest, hoping to change not only myself but the lives of half the world, a parishioner said to me: 'In your life if you succeed in changing just a little part of yourself, you will have achieved a great deal.' I now know that he was right.

I am restricted by my self-image and the expectations I think other people lay on me. Much of this is of my own generating. Past failings and hurts seem to cling, firmly but unseen, like barnacles to the bottom of a ship. I do not always recognise the pride which tempts me to act in a way that raises self-esteem and wins approval, but wastes God's precious grace. Fear of criticism, rejection or failure can cripple my desires to branch out in new directions, and ability to change can be impeded by an instinct to rely on myself rather than risk 'losing my life'.

This is compounded by not trusting God enough and not taking him at his word. God is faithful. I have frequently experienced his total and unconditional love, in my own life and in others, especially when it was least deserved. He promises that he 'will free his people' – which includes me. Yet, like Paul, I cry out in powerlessness, again and again: 'Who will rescue me, wretched man that I am?' Gratefully my heart responds: 'Thanks be to God, through Jesus Christ, my Lord' (Rom. 7:24).

I do not share the view of many who see powerlessness as a negative denial of opportunity, frustration or hindrance to the realisation of potential. God has touched me with his saving grace in many experiences of powerlessness. He allows me to experience powerlessness – as in my inability to trust his promises. It is a kind of 'sting in the flesh', a reminder of my lack of humility and my dependence on him. 'The glory of God' can come through any incident, no matter how painful, as in the death of Lazarus. Calling on God when I am weak, vulnerable, or hurting, frees him to shed his light, speak the necessary word of wisdom, and do what is needed. When powerless, I can experience God's saving power and the fulfilment of Scripture in my life: 'The Spirit comes to help us in our weakness' (Rom. 8:26) and the goodness of Jesus promises that 'I will not leave you orphans, I will come to you' (John 14:18).

People struggling with difficulties, perhaps recurring temptations or sins which they cannot overcome or eliminate, often come to me for help. No longer am I lured into offering the fruitless advice others have given to me: 'You must accept this as part of your life; it is not going to change.' While we all have our weaknesses and cannot overcome them ourselves, yet with God *nothing is impossible, and all is possible.* The Spirit uses my struggles to give God glory. He draws good out of all things. He can empower me to trust him more through begging him to use my struggles *for those* who come to me for ministry.

Jesus did not answer St Paul's prayer directly by taking away the thorn in his flesh, but gave him something better: 'My grace is sufficient for you.' Efforts to act out of grace give God more glory perhaps than his removing my specific thorn. Most of us want to act out of our own strength rather than God's. Wouldn't it be delightful – sometimes anyway – to come before God, not so powerless, saying, 'Lord, see this . . . which I have done for you'? This is an illusion built on pride, satisfying self, and a temptation to act in independence of God. The enemy is wily and we can easily deceive ourselves – nowhere, perhaps, more than in this question of power and powerlessness, independence and dependence on God.

Identifying myself as a sinner amongst sinful people puzzles many of our contemporaries. The modern view of sin is continually narrowing. Whatever appears not to harm another and is between consenting adults is deemed all right. Sin is not seen as the rejection of God's love by a disordered heart which may later be manifested in wrong actions. The heart can be 'a treacherous place' (Ps. 64) harbouring both good and evil. We had a fine custom in priestly training, which still helps me. We used to pray, silently in our hearts, Psalm 51 – David's great psalm of repentance and conversion following his adultery with Bathsheba and later the planned murder of her husband, Uriah, to cover up his sin. The words 'a pure heart create for me, O God, put a steadfast spirit within me' have long been at the heart of my prayer, purifying and strengthening me.

Fr George Kosiki at a priests' retreat at Manchester in 1978 said: 'All of us here are sinners; if you are not a sinner, or do not believe yourself to be a sinner, you had better go home now, for God has nothing to offer you. Jesus Christ came to save sinners.'

The priest at the end of my receiving the sacrament of reconciliation once said to me, 'Father, you are acquitted.' I then had a very clear image of myself being charged, and being found guilty. However, though guilty, I was acquitted, let off. This brought home to me – in a way that is engraved in my heart – the awareness that, though a sinner, I have been acquitted because of the love of Jesus Christ who purifies me with his blood.

Being convicted and convinced of personal sinfulness is a great grace. Unable to save myself, a sinner, does not leave me condemned, but glorifying Christ Jesus my Redeemer and Lord. 'I will praise you, Lord, you have rescued me. You have not let my enemy rejoice over me' (Ps. 30:8). Thanks be to God, through Christ Jesus, my Lord.

It is also necessary to look at power and its use by Christ, 'to whom all authority in heaven on earth has been given' (Matt. 28:18). Wisdom and selflessness are required to use power constructively, not destructively. Christ is our model for the right use of power. He did not use power to save himself but surrendered himself voluntarily to his enemies. He rejects kingship as a sign of power, and challenges disciples who seek power as to whether they can drink his cup of suffering. He reassures those who fear loneliness of his constant presence saying, 'you will be clothed with power from on high' (Luke. 24:49). The Holy Spirit is the power, the source of all holiness, the sanctifier who strengthens us in powerlessness.

I remember offering my mind, heart, soul and will to the Lord. Hurts I experienced as a youngster surfaced the next day. Suddenly not only did I not want to forgive those who had treated me unjustly, but I wanted them punished. Totally powerless and unable to move my mind, heart or even desire to forgive, I was in spiritual paralysis. Looking to the powerless Lord nailed on the crucifix, I groaned: 'Lord, yesterday I gave you my mind, my heart and my will. Today I can't even use them to forgive. Take, Lord, my mind, heart and will and use them to forgive for me.' That was what Jesus did!

He empowered me with forgiveness and I experienced great healing. When it is difficult to cope, in a Christian way, with situations, incidents, or people, I pray repeatedly: 'Jesus bless . . .' (naming the person or situation).

The whole thing is resolved by Jesus. The continuous invocation of the all holy and powerful name of Jesus never fails to transform attitudes, people and situations, for 'all power is given in Jesus' name'.

God speaks powerfully to me through his word in the Bible. He can lead to the right word for certain situations, give helpful insight to another's state of mind or soul, and provide direction according to his will. The word of God is power-full in the sacrament of reconciliation, giving strength and divine wisdom.

Years ago I made a key commitment to the Lord to go to the sacrament of reconciliation weekly. Tremendous would my loss have been if I had not used this sacrament, which helps me to forgive as I am forgiven. Moreover, God gives grace, light and direction for the coming week through enfolding me in his love and power in this sacrament.

My 'feet of clay' will always be with me but Christ has freed me from much hard-heartedness, from emotional and spiritual deadness which kills joy and stymies growth. Daily I pray: 'O that today you would listen to his voice, harden not your heart' (Ps. 94) and 'a pure heart create for me, O God'. There is no spiritual bypass surgery for clogged hearts. The divine physician heals all. Through powerlessness he draws me to his love. Daily, may I surrender more to him, praising, glorifying and thanking him for all that he has done, is doing and will continue to do in me, so that he can use me for his beloved people.

My soul glorifies the Lord,
My spirit rejoices in God, my Saviour,
The Almighty has done great things for me,
Holy is his name. (Luke 1: 46–55).

A TIME FOR PRAYER

Sandra Murphy

Sandra Murphy is twenty-two and lives in Dublin. She is studying to become a chartered accountant and is working as an auditor while she completes her training.

Sandra's faith in God was strong enough to keep her attending Mass when her friends ceased to attend. Still she found it boring. She also gradually discovered that while she was maturing at other levels of her being, this was not true in her spiritual life. Fortunately, a friend introduced her to a lively group of young people led by a Franciscan. Her thirst for God led her further still to another group. In Light out of Darkness, she was challenged to know herself, to claim her frailties and to develop a deeper relationship with Christ. She discovered, experientially, the power of the body of Christ and a deeper intimacy with Christ. As a result, Sandra discovered the power of the Mass which began to transform her whole life.

K.O'S.

With every generation there is a movement. For my parents it was flower power and hippies. For me it was watching my friends drifting away from the church.

When I was young it was part of my routine to get up early on a Sunday morning, meet my friends and go to Mass. It was a trial not to chatter to each other but we made an effort and restrained ourselves. We monitored our watches constantly but every second seemed like a minute. Finally, the Mass was over and our duty was done for another week.

As I got older a few of my friends decided that by going to Mass they were not getting to know God better and that they were learning nothing more about him; so gradually they ceased going. As a result of this, I became isolated in my beliefs. It was difficult to talk to friends who did not have the same feelings because there is such a fine line between confiding and preaching. However, I believed in God and I continued attending Mass because of this faith in him.

One evening, a friend asked me to go to a youth group with her as she had arranged to meet someone there and did not want to arrive alone. It was not until we were walking to the meeting that she revealed to me that this was a religious group. Imagine my shock and horror. As with many people of my age, I believed that these religious meetings were only for priests and nuns. Nobody I knew ever went. However, I decided to give it a try.

The group was a youth group that met weekly and was run by the Franciscans. It was made up of individuals aged from seventeen to twenty-five years of age. At the meeting, the gospel for the coming Sunday was read and then passed to everyone in the group. We were all asked to share our feelings about the passage. It did not have to be much, just a word or a line from the reading.

I did not feel comfortable enough to contribute to the meeting but I listened. I was amazed that the other participants were so vocal and even more amazed that so much of what they said reflected my own thoughts and feelings.

The following week I went to the meeting again, but this time by myself. I tried to concentrate on the gospel. To my surprise it related to my own life. I started to share my feelings and listened more intently to others. These meetings helped me to realise that the weekly Mass had something to say to me through the gospel.

I had been attending these young Franciscan meetings for a number of years when I began to feel that I was saying the same thing again and again. I felt that I was maturing normally at the human level, but my religious beliefs were not developing at the same pace.

On the advice of the one of the friars, I decided to join a group called 'Light out of Darkness', based on a book by Kathleen O'Sullivan which was used by groups throughout Ireland and England for the purpose of sharing faith and enriching our relationship with God.

The groups normally met once a week for ten weeks and each meeting had a different theme relating to day-to-day situations and emotions. The chosen theme was expanded on during the meetings using extracts from the Bible. We were asked to reflect on these thoughts for the coming week and then at a later stage to share our feelings.

One of the main requirements of the course was to try to spend at least fifteen minutes a day praying to God. I had considered myself well acquainted with God. I spent at least a couple of hours each week in his company (between going to Mass and going to my youth group). Thus when I first heard that I had to spend fifteen minutes praying to him, I never even thought about it. I assumed that it would be simply an extension of my daily prayers. I was never more wrong.

The first week I had great difficulty. What was I to say or talk about? Until then most of my praying had taken the form of the standard Hail Mary and Our Father. Can you imagine how many Hail Marys and Our Fathers you can fit into fifteen minutes? I had never before realised how stereotyped my praying had become. I was so stuck for words that I had to start off by splitting the fifteen minutes into two sessions of seven and a half minutes each. I was amazed to discover how hard it was. I had attended Mass all my life and said my prayers every day, and yet I had nothing to say to my God. I experienced shock!

However, I persevered with my praying, and gradually, it became easier. As time went by, I found that I could easily spend the fifteen minutes and sometimes longer talking to God and sharing with Him the thoughts, ideas and sensations that I shared with friends. As our relationship progressed, I realised that I had never before had a relationship with God. Now, through my daily prayers, I had started to build one until, as with an age-old friend, I could talk to him, in a disjointed manner in my own words without using the structure of traditional prayers.

Ecclesiastes says, 'There is a season for everything, a time for every occupation under heaven'. The writer goes on to list many activities and emotions that he feels are necessary in everyday life. One that I feel he missed, but is just as necessary, is prayer. I spent years thinking that I was religious and that I had a good relationship with God only to discover that I had never known him at all. Light out of Darkness taught me the necessity of communicating with God daily, and about the ordinary events of that day.

Every relationship needs communication on a regular basis or it disintegrates. If I don't see or talk to my friends on a regular basis, the ease with which we used to converse is gone. When we meet again the words bubble out as I remember different things that have occurred since we last met. Then the well dries up. We have grown apart and have lost the common ground that made us friends.

The same applies to my relationship with God. I used to think that going to Mass on a Sunday and saying my prayers each night was enough, but I had been hiding behind the age-old prayers and words, and not communicating with God at all. I never told him anything about my personal life. I never told him anything about the things that were important to me. Since I started praying daily, I have recognised the difference in our relationship. I am now more inclined to confide in God and talk to him at all sorts of times and places, and to listen to him as well! That takes some getting used to, but it comes.

Each time I felt that I was becoming closer to God, he threw another challenge at me that showed me how far I still had to go. Every time I become frustrated and feel that my belief is going nowhere, God, in his own way, shows me the next step to take.

Even recently, he helped me. I was finding it difficult to fit in all my activities. I was working long hours. I was only able to attend one training session out of two each week for sport and it had been weeks since I had talked to some of my friends. I decided that I really had to cut back on some activities. I decided I would continue praying each day, but Mass once a fortnight would have to suffice.

On my way home from Mass one day soon afterwards, I met a stranger of my own age. We began talking and he told me that it was the first time he had attended Mass in three years. He was full of joy and found it difficult to believe that attending Mass could have had such a profound effect on him. He told me that he tried to talk to God regularly but that he had not felt his presence for a long time. Today, however, he had felt close to him. In the face of this, I realised my mistake.

God's home is the church. It is the place which is dedicated to his presence. I feel more confident in my home and I am more free in my speech and expressions there. Why should it surprise me that God is too; that he would find it easier to confide and talk to us in his own surroundings? Or is it that his presence in his home, the church, affects us and we share his feelings more deeply there? As in the case of my stranger, I too have sometimes found it easier to speak to God when I am surrounded by his presence which pervades the church.

While I was growing up, the 'church' was a regular topic of conversation. I discussed it with friends, its structure and how right or wrong it was. We debated whether going to church was necessary or not. Surely one could be a good Christian without the necessity of going to Mass? We tended to think that the Catholic values we were taught should be put into practice on a full-time basis and that they were not affected by our spending three-quarters of an hour each week at a service in which we did not participate. However, it is easy to think that we are being good Catholics by behaving well; but by praying and attending Mass we are worshipping our God. Then we recognise truly God's true place – Creator, Saviour, the one who makes holy – and we learn to see that, as sinners, we are lost without him. Besides, our relationship with God is all about love, his selfless love, my limited love. But it can develop and the power comes from God.

Thus I feel that if I am willing to make the time, God is willing to show me the way. He has taught me that it is not the celebration of Mass alone that develops a relationship. There is much more to it than that, and we can learn a lot about how to let God love us and how to love him in return by looking at good *human* relationships. The Mass is God's total giving in love to save me – as he has done. Through a deeper understanding of the Mass, I am helped by God to understand better the selflessness of loving. This is why my friends, other people, are so important to me. Often I have to be more gentle, more understanding with others whom I may not really like much, but I keep learning two things: God comes very close to me when I try, in faith, to find him in other people and when I let him somehow – in me – give me the desire and the strength to persevere in doing that; and I get the strength and the faith and the love to do that – and often it is a struggle – through the Mass.

Prayer (talking to God about all the little things as well as the bigger things) is my lifeline; the Mass is my sharing in the great sacrifice and prayer of Jesus to his Father on behalf of me and of you. It gives meaning to my little sacrifices. It gives meaning to my life!

PRAYER CHANGES PEOPLE

Elisabeth Tuttle

Elisabeth Tuttle is a native of Stradbally, in Ireland. She has taught mainly in England, holding the post of head of religious departments in two comprehensive schools before becoming religious education adviser to Catholic schools in the archdiocese of Birmingham. Elizabeth was a part-time prison chaplain for many years. At present she is involved in Light out of Darkness retreats and in the Maranatha Community's spiritual programmes.

Elisabeth is an experienced woman of prayer, an able leader of groups and committed to working with the marginalised – especially prisoners. Her testimony of faith in God's fidelity to the marginalised is deeply moving. 'At that prayer meeting . . . I experienced Christ as with his body, all of us with no distinctions, all being cherished and loved . . . he seemed to shepherd us as a little flock', writes Elisabeth. Without condoning the crimes in any way, she felt she was clearly taught that no child of God is ever beyond redemption.

K.O'S.

Having spent a great number of years in the teaching profession my little world mainly revolved around children, parents, parish and my religious community. But shortly before I was due to take early retirement my eyes were opened to a very different kind of world. This happened when I found myself within prison walls ministering to male prisoners. A Christian friend who had been asked to lead a prison mission required a woman on his team and asked me to consider prayerfully this most unexpected and challenging request. I had arrived at that stage in my spiritual life where I had come to know that total surrender to God's will was the best and only way to true peace and happiness. I tried to discern in prayer what the Lord wanted regarding this mission. His touch in my spirit was so gentle and peaceful that I knew my response was a willing 'Yes'.

I went into the prison nevertheless with quite a measure of fear and trepidation. Soon I began to realise I was the privileged one when so many inmates frankly, openly, and with such trust, began relating to me. It was a memorable and moving experience for me when a group of thirty prisoners gathered in a circle around us at a prayer meeting. All of them, without exception, asked the Anglican minister and me to pray with them for their individual needs. Tears flowed in abundance, tears of repentance, tears of joy, releasing and healing tears. The presence of a compassionate Jesus was close to us. Some shared how the Lord was touching them.

Afterwards one said brokenly, 'I was a con-man, but not any more; I have seen the Lord, I believe.' Before we left, the Anglican clergyman asked God and the men for forgiveness, confessing that he had indeed been guilty of thinking that his coming into a prison for a week's mission would be a waste of his time! God had convicted him of his blindness. Personally, I was deeply moved and aware of many prejudices in my thinking. 'Your thoughts are not my thoughts' from Isaiah were a reproach to me. The gospel came alive in a meaningful way for me. Jesus seems always 'at home' among social outcasts. The *anawim*, the marginalised, the sinners seem to have a special place in his heart. His presence among us at that prayer meeting was very powerful. I experienced Christ as with his body, all of us with no distinctions, all being cherished and loved. We were one because we were together in his name and he seemed to shepherd us as a little flock, setting an example of how to love one another.

Fortunately I was allowed to keep up contact with a number of these men on a weekly basis. I started a prayer group for prisoners which was also attended by an outside group of Christian men, together with a Bible study group. Who gained most, I wonder, from these groups that prayed together, humbly acknowledging their total dependence on Christ? It certainly restored a measure of dignity to the prisoners; and to me much needed truth and humility. My gratitude overflowed.

One evening when the leaders of the Bible study group and I arrived at the prison gate, it was explained that for certain reasons, there could not be a prayer meeting that evening. We were, however, readily granted our request to go to the chapel for our own prayer experience. As we prayed together we felt that the Holy Spirit was moving us to *listen* deeply. The upshot of this meeting without the prisoners was that God's love for them led us to see that we could support prisoners not only by the established prayer meeting in the prison, but by a meeting in our neighbourhood which would pray for the needs and well-being of the prisoners. Within a few days, these Christian men and their wives joined me in our convent. There we prayed for about two hours holding up to the Lord prisoners both known and unknown to us. Again we experienced the closeness and the power of God. Nor was that the end of the story! God's generosity went further!

On the following Sunday I felt urged to join my Christian colleagues at the prison, something I didn't normally do. As we chatted to inmates over a cup of tea a colleague called me over to where he was chatting to three *radiant* prisoners. He asked them to explain again to me what had happened to them. The evening we had prayed in our convent these three prisoners were together in a cell listening to a radio. They were *not* members of our prison prayer group which makes it all the more remarkable! Suddenly they felt an awesome presence in their midst. They were startled but somehow they knew it was all right; they knew it was the Lord, though they didn't know how, and they immediately began to pray. What followed sounded like something one reads about in the Acts of the Apostles! Their hearts burned within them – they knew they were loved by God, as the Holy Spirit filled them with his peace and joy. This inner radiance still lit their faces on the Sunday when I heard their story. The Holy Spirit had touched their lives. They joined our prayer group later.

One of these men was in prison for murder and for rape. Consequently he was given a rough time by fellow inmates. Sometime later at a prayer meeting I had to fight back the tears, as he simply and sincerely prayed for his attackers. Some months later he was moved to another prison where he expected to undergo the same rough treatment. One day I received a letter from him. It filled me with joy. He wrote:

My problems and difficulties soon became second place as I found myself becoming actively involved in sharing in service with fellow Christians. You know, before no time at all I found myself rejoicing in an inner peace which was new to me. I had never known that problems too disappeared. The Lord had just washed me clean – all the former treatment was a kind of preparation, a remoulding period. I wanted what I had seen in others and now it became and is mine – peace of mind in the Lord Jesus Christ, able to praise his name at all times and to have a living relationship with him. I feel so different.

From that time on I became convinced of the power of intercessory prayer when members of the body of Christ meet to hold up to the Lord other wounded members of his broken body.

This man's experience was one of the many lessons I learned through my prison ministry. Though the Lord never allowed me to condone the crimes committed or forget the suffering caused to victims and their families, yet he showed me clearly that no son of his was ever beyond redemption, though it does require sincere repentance on the part of the criminal.

In the years that followed no matter what town or city I was moved to by my superiors, there was always a prison near by. So I gained experience in almost every kind of Her Majesty's penal establishments! The most challenging was a top security prison, where I was asked to help start a prayer group – one which was well attended. Some of the participants became evangelists among their own fellow inmates. That was inspiring to us leaders. Eventually I was officially appointed a part-time voluntary chaplain, and to my great surprise I was allocated keys. This gave me freedom of movement around the prison where often I would encounter some of the toughest criminals in the country, but also those who proved later to be victims of a miscarriage of justice. Some of these I knew well and was convinced of their innocence. Personally, I recognised that *prisoners* were setting me free. I was learning to look fearlessly at my own faults, rash judgments and self-protection measures. God walked with me on those long corridors. As I moved from place to place my fearlessness surprised even myself. I recognised that what I was doing I could only do in the strength of the Lord and not in my own great weakness. My friends no longer regarded me as the little 'dove' they used to know but teasingly remarked on my sprouting eagle's wings! In prisons I came to know myself better and to know and love my God more truly and more genuinely.

In the segregation unit in this particular top security prison was a 'lifer' whom I got to know. Though he was believed to be the most violent man in the prison, he treated me with respect. One day shortly after he had received the very sad news that his young niece, whom he obviously loved, had been murdered, he asked if I could come to see him. When I sat down to speak to him I saw a changed person. He exuded hatred and destructive anger. Although this was not directed against me, I felt utterly helpless and even fearful. While I was listening I was also praying that somehow the Lord would step into this hopeless situation, because I was powerless. God did not fail me. He never fails a heart that trusts. As the man stood up to leave, he handed me as a gift a piece of parchment on which he had printed in beautiful calligraphy the Breastplate of St Patrick. I admired his work and thanked him sincerely. Then unexpectedly I felt prompted to say, calling him by name, 'You have given me a beautiful gift; I, too, would like to offer you a gift if you are willing to accept it.' Quite surprised he waited to hear what it was. 'If you are willing, I can pray with you for your niece, Vicky, whom you truly love. I promise you, it will help Vicky and you too. Are you willing?' He agreed.

I began by consecrating his *imagination* to the Lord, while at the same time saying in the depths of my heart, 'Lord, you have helped me get this far; over to you now, please, to do the rest and to bring healing to this poor man whom you love.' Soon this tough angry man was sobbing. When I had finished I asked if anything special had happened during the prayer. 'Yes', he replied, 'I saw Vicky and she smiled at me.' He never remembered crying before, but in the days that followed he cried many, many tears. When I next met him a week later he was transformed. He greeted me with a handshake and calmly he said, 'All the hate has left me. It seems to have been washed away with my tears.' This may seem incredible to you who read, but it happened. I personally believe the Lord worked a miracle in the soul of that man, who loved his niece and grieved for her. Genuine love, which has the hallmark of selflessness, always bears fruit. Prayer is powerful to change people. Much depends on the intercessory prayer, so we must never give up praying for others, hoping and trusting in God.

My experience over and over again, no matter what part of the world I am in, is that God's love reaches out to save if only hearts open to receive. Some years ago I was invited by American friends to the States, in order to address various Christian groups. The organisers decided it would be a good idea for me to visit the local women's jail, but I hadn't brought my prison identity card with me. Minutes after the idea had been abandoned I came across the *number* of my identity card in my Bible – how I found it there I do not know! Once again the Lord opened the door for me to meet prisoners; the identity card number satisfied the authorities and I managed two visits. The women asked for a healing service. During that service it was obvious from their faces that the Lord was moving them. Tears flowed; the atmosphere changed. I heard one woman cry out, 'I don't want to go on the streets again; I really don't; God strengthen me, help me!'

Later that evening I was brought to a half-way house for drug addicts where I myself was blessed by a special anointing of the Holy Spirit. I knew God gave me this gift so that it might reach others there. The power of the Spirit seemed to overwhelm all who prayed. As one girl got up she gleefully said, 'I'm on a high; I'm on a high!' Her joy was obvious. We all knew the kind of Spirit-filled 'high' she was talking about. There would be no withdrawal symptoms that night!

Apart from these prison experiences where I have

personally witnessed and been graced by the presence of God, active and alive in other people, I would like to share here the importance I place on the richness of presence in the body of Christ. We are all links in that body. We can build up or weaken one another. The strength of each link fills the whole body with God's presence. This is why Christ's teaching on our neighbour is so valuable. A *smile* that warms another strengthens each link, and Christ is the heart of every chain. When I feel too tired to do more than smile at people, I believe Christ receives the smile as my prayer.

Through my American friends I became linked with the Maranatha Community (an interdenominational community which puts great emphasis on 'equipping the saints' [Eph. 4:12], so that members will be more effective where they live, work and worship). I have experienced the power of God's presence not only at their gatherings in England but also on pilgrimages to what was then Czechoslovakia and to Northern Ireland. Even though we were gathered from many Christian traditions I have witnessed barriers being broken down, prejudices disappearing. I have witnessed miracles of reconciliation and forgiveness because of the unifying force of the Lord's presence in the midst of his body – his people who are gathered in his name. All of this reveals how vital prayer is to bind us all together, to encourage and support one another and to recognise in truth that we ourselves can always change and grow and develop as passionate lovers of the great God who loved us first.

UNEXPECTED FREEDOM

Barbara Bolton

Barbara Bolton is a married Catholic with three grown-up children. She is active in a number of ministries: as a Christian listening tutor, a leader in human-spiritual growth programmes based on Light out of Darkness; as an apostolate member of the Acorn Christian Healing Trust; and as a lay auditor of a diocesan marriage tribunal.

In Barbara's testimony – as in that of others – a member of Christ's body, and a group or cell of that same body, became the way into a deeper knowing of herself and a more intimate relationship with Christ. Barbara experienced healing from hurts in the past which had crippled her emotionally, depriving her of confidence. She experienced the unexpected release from a poor self-image and the gift of freedom which opened her to a ministry to others, a precious gift from God.

K.O'S.

Some years ago, in a parish served by Benedictines, I

attended a talk on the role of the laity in the church of the future based on a publication called *A Time for Building*, its title taken from the verses in Ecclesiastes 3 beginning 'There is a season for everything'. By coincidence I had been given a copy only days before by a member of the working party that produced it. Twenty years previously Sr Kathleen Lawson had been my headmistress and very significant in my life. Now I was married with three children while she had recently started a 'small community' project in London where we had a joyful reunion. After the talk one monk, Fr Nicholas, when asked his opinion on lay involvement, spoke of spiritual renewal, beginning with prayer rather than mere church maintenance. More questions and discussion led to our taking out diaries and arranging a date to meet.

These seemingly small events were to be used by God to transform the whole direction of my life, transform its quality, transform my inner core. Thus began my journey into true freedom, into learning to listen like a disciple. This is quite breathtaking even now after many years of personal experience and reflection.

We met regularly to pray, to reflect on Scripture and to share its relevance to our everyday life. A growing awareness of something deeper, something attractive, drew me on. The momentum faded, however; doubts were expressed about our readiness through prayer for a new release of the Spirit. Personally I felt both disappointed and deprived, surely God would have given us something! Before long the meetings ended.

I resisted groups for a long time, not wanting a repeat experience. In my heart I had gone off God, who seemed beyond reach. In my teens a developing prayer life had a transforming effect on my behaviour, which could be disruptive and attention-seeking. I struggled with a suggested religious vocation; this was misunderstood and dismissed at home as religious mania. Home life was full of demands and incredible pressures. Relationships were volatile. My spiritual diet needed more of God, the real God. Only later I recognised that my human self also needed wise attention from experienced people.

Career plans ended abruptly after a sudden parental decision meant my leaving school to work with my father, who was almost blind and in failing health. There really was no option. Two years under great stress and responsibility took its toll. Sr Kathleen Lawson, still in contact, recognised the signs of an approaching breakdown and fortunately intervened. And God, where was he for me? In my immense need and woundedness I clung to him and knew somehow he was there, giving me courage to make a move. I went to France working as an *au pair* at a school in the countryside, and life stabilised again. Peace returned and with it health. Sadly within months of returning home, my father died. I felt bereft. Through all this I poured out my heart and grief to God.

Life went on, and gradually mine took another happier direction with a career, then marriage and motherhood. The Lord's voice dimmed; more truthfully, my hearing diminished. In my heart I thought I had refused his call. Until now. All these years later I was to learn of the faithfulness of God, 'underneath are the everlasting arms'.

When a friend shared the renewal of her faith with me, I responded to her offer to lend me a book. To my surprise it gripped me; I read avidly. The desire for a deeper relationship with God surfaced again. This time I did some serious asking, repeatedly praying aloud: 'Come Holy Spirit, enkindle in me the fire of your love.'

Venturing into unknown territory aroused apprehension, but the desire to move through any barrier was stronger than doubt or fear. After a very long time, exhausted, I stopped.

Love drew me on. I phoned Fr Nicholas and begged for help. Promising prayer support ('I'll pray all day') he asked if anyone could pray with me. Love provided; that day at an ecumenical group a friend prayed with the laying-on-of-hands and asked God to fill me to overflowing with his Spirit, 'a full measure, pressed down, shaken together, and running over'. I experienced great peace and immense joy. Returning home 'on a high' I made arrangements to restart our prayer group. Then, whilst gazing at the beauty of the spring flowers in the garden, I was overwhelmed with a powerful and totally unexpected sense of release. I found myself weeping; the tears just flowed. I had so bottled up my emotions that they seemed not to have life any more. Now they were released by the fire of God's love. I felt charged, energised with the presence of his Spirit.

Through the gift of the Spirit the word of God became alive and active, and there was a terrible thirst in me for more and more. I could not live again in the arid land I had known, I was out of prison. I trusted in God and became happily dependent on him who had brought me new life. Through the presence and power of the Holy Spirit, a whole new life is possible.

Light shone in the darkness and with it came change. I had allowed a poor self-image and a spirit of timidity to choke the voice of God within. Freedom allowed new relationships with other parts of the body of Christ. It was the support I needed. Where I had avoided involvement, I now longed to get involved. One immediate way was responding to the crisis that was then besetting Poland. By co-operating together we despatched clothing direct to parishes and convents. It was arduous, exhausting but wonderful when unexpected letters arrived full of gratitude to God who had moved our hearts to provide for their need; it was humbling.

But was there a danger that I would become lost in busyness for God, spending energy, but letting my heart, love and humanity dry up and wither again. Yet, God was watchful and the advocate whom Jesus had promised to send to 'teach everything' came alongside me and my fellow workers. The prayer group we started grew and was a source of renewal and healing for many. As this love relationship with God grew so did our awareness of pain. The pain I carried from hurts and wounds of the past, which were deeply buried within me, surfaced. In amazing ways I became healed and gradually I became more sensitive to pain in others.

Like the Samaritan woman, I drew on the living water within that Jesus speaks about. Love changed my attitude to others, reflected in my more caring, more selfless approach. I discovered a gift of 'hospitality of heart' as a listener. Some, who came to me and shared, drank together with me at the well of living water that kept rising up within us. The Spirit of God was abroad, alive and active. A 'new thing' was happening in us and between us. We marvelled at the presence and power of the Lord.

New life, shared with others who had likewise risen out of darkness, brought new wisdom. The closer God drew me and shed his light the clearer I saw, recognised and claimed the truth. I knew I needed deeper *healing* as my deeply hidden wounds could still cause me agony. In

God's light I saw I needed to *forgive* many who had injured me. I forgave and it cost mightily. With forgiveness came healing: 'And when you stand in prayer, forgive whatever you have against anybody, so that the Father in heaven may forgive your failings too' (Mark 11:25).

I brought to God the areas of my life where I had felt shattered, rejected, almost annihilated, and on the receiving end of deep anger. I asked God's help to forgive the perpetrators from my heart; to help me to let go of feelings of bitter resentment and injustice and in their place to fill me with his love and forgiveness. I begged out of my helplessness, powerlessness and deep longing. I discovered an inner healing power in the sacrament of reconciliation through Fr Nicholas's special 'ministry of listening'. This led to the healing that Paul speaks of in Ephesians 3:14: 'may he give you the power through his Spirit for your hidden self to grow strong' (this was the healing of my soul – the innermost part of *my personality*) 'so that Christ may live in your hearts through faith.' This inner healing, I believe, has allowed me the freedom to become more the person God created in love, who is made in his image and likeness, that is growing in his wisdom, his kindness, his love. This prayer of Paul's became my daily prayer and the charter of freedom by which I tried to live.

In the years since, gratitude for my freedom has manifested a willingness to serve God, and follow where he has led. 'Glory be to him whose power, working in us, can do infinitely more than we can ask or imagine . . . in the Church and in Christ Jesus for ever and ever. Amen' (Eph. 3:20).

RICHES OF THE HEART

Kathryn Coakley

Kathryn Coakley is a Yorkshire girl who moved to Ireland with her husband in 1973 and taught in a boys' school for twenty-three years. She is now diocesan religious adviser (special education) for primary education, and director of formation for the secular Franciscan Order and vice-president of its eastern regional council.

Kathryn's testimony is a genuine expression of deep faith in the tender love of God for all sinners who wholeheartedly beg his mercy. We can easily become over-busy, leaving little time for honest reflection, and so can fall into the trap of self-deception. The experience, however, of God's forgiveness and love is such that Kathryn says from her heart: 'I'm learning to treasure those times of darkness.' It is then, as we learn, that the Lord disciplines those whom he loves.

K.O'S.

A frozen embryo, a bird in a gilded cage, a butterfly

in chrysalis form – such was I. Something was absent, something not right. There had to be more to this matter of religion than saying my prayers, prayers offered to a God out there in infinity, removed from my experience.

The Cloud of Unknowing says, 'By love he can be caught and held, but by thinking never.' This had to be the key. I hope I've embarked on a journey into the infinite riches of the heart of my God. I beg him to teach me each day a little of the richness of his love, the many facets of his love. This is the heart I seek to know. A heart that is an abyss of love, so little understood. A heart weighed down with love for the sinner that he will stop at nothing to go in search of the lost sheep. Such a one was I.

> He pulled me out of the horrible pit
> Out of the slough of the marsh
> He has settled my feet on a rock
> And steadied my steps.

(Ps. 40)

Yes, I can humbly acknowledge my need of God in my life. I am very far from perfect, yet I know I am a *loved* sinner. There are many times I fail him bitterly yet I know that if I turn to him in sorrow, his forgiveness is instantaneous. My response must be one of contrition to obtain the outflow of his forgiveness. The quality of his forgiveness is something that I need to grow in knowledge of. It's reflected in his patient tenderness with me. What he is seeking from me is the love of my heart, however feeble that may be, in response to his own boundless love. God's indulgent love towards me is beyond my understanding. With the psalmist, I can say:

My sin is always before me
Against you alone have I sinned
What is evil in your sight I have done.

(Ps. 51)

It reminds me of my rightful place before him. I may often have to present myself before him as the 'unprofitable servant without means to pay'. When I humble myself and ask for the forgiveness of his heart, then it is that he covers me with his seamless white robe. Indeed his mercy is as if our sins had never been, if we can place our trust in him.

Trusting God has not always been easy. For so long in the past I held him aloof, not really letting him have front seat in the car, just letting him be a back-seat passenger. I was very much in control. I was still the centre of my little universe. I kept such a tight hold of the steering wheel that nothing could prise it from my hands.

He watched me as I went on hurtling into destruction, my world crashing around me before I finally capitulated. I had had enough of being in control. It was through the profound darkness that real light came into my life. That darkness without resources was the darkness of my own sinfulness. Until that moment, pride had blinded me from seeing the need of my Saviour in my life. But the tender love of the heart of my God was only too ready to salvage me from the wreckage of my head-on-collision. What a relief when I finally let him count for something real in my life. I was able to utter a prayer: 'Lord, I never knew you loved me so much.' From that moment, the scales of self-deception fell from my eyes. I saw my need for forgiveness for all the sin in my life; my need for healing;

my need for God to save me from myself. It's a healing that goes on each day of all that is unworthy in me, unworthy of the love-relationship which he offers me. How humble is my God!

Amazingly, I'm learning to treasure those times of darkness. Through the darkness, he reveals to me those aspects of my life that displease him, that must be transformed. I no longer become angry or tempestuously impatient with myself, because I am learning that the Lord disciplines those he loves. Everything comes from his loving hands as he seeks to transform my rebellious and unruly heart into a resting place for him. 'I will take out your heart of stone and give you a heart of flesh.'

Under the gentle and tender touch that is his, yet also challenging, I'm being led to a deeper understanding of his unfailing love despite my unutterable weakness and failure. In fact, these are the very things which draw him to me. 'Do those who are well need a doctor?'

The darkness in my life – be it sin, failure, disappointment, setback, anxiety, fear – can all be used as a springboard to make a leap of trust and surrender, as I learn to say, 'May your will be done.' Like some precious jewel or stone, he cuts and carves and forms me into the shape he has in mind, saying always, 'You are precious in my eyes.'

I do not have to wait to be perfect to experience his love in my life. Like St Paul, 'I want to boast all the more about my weaknesses so that the power of Christ may dwell in me and be experienced by me.' I'm beginning to glimpse that this change in attitude in me, of coming before him in my poverty, is the key that opens the door to release the flood that is his love. It is only when I can accept that I am nothing, that he is everything, that I come to experience the truth that enlightens and sets free. Alone I can do nothing. I am dependent on him for everything. I can now rejoice in that reality! I am like a child and I need to find again those childlike qualities of trust, docility and simplicity. Then I can expect all from him, who delights in nurturing me.

> I praise you Lord my God with all my heart
> And glorify your name forever
> For your love to me has been great
> You have saved me from the depths of the grave.

(Ps. 85)

FORGIVING MYSELF

John Murphy

John Murphy is a Dubliner, married to Philomena, and they have three young children. He is a lecturer in computer science at Dublin City University and specialises in ongoing research into software engineering. He is currently a project leader in a research programme funded by the EC.

John writes honestly: 'My faith at this time was threadbare as is the faith of many people in the modern world.' An admission of truth like that is taking a stand on firm ground, on the rock that is Christ. It draws down the compassion and love of God, as happened in John's case. He began to see the truth more clearly and was released from false guilt. This marked the 'turning-point' in a new relationship with Christ. His thirst for prayer, his desire to know God deeply mark the beginning of a journey into the kingdom for himself and for others.

K.O'S.

When I wrote the first draft of this article I had great

difficulty in selecting an appropriate title. I thought that the article was about my forgiving my father so I called it 'Forgiving my Father'. Deeper insight revealed that, in fact, I was writing about forgiving myself. What then do I want to forgive myself for? Let me begin with a memory.

I am lying like a stone in my bed. I am six or seven years old and it is winter time. I know that it is winter time because my bed, which is a bunk above my younger brother's, is covered with coats. He is asleep and I am awake. Rigid with fear I listen, as I do on many nights, to my parents arguing. The sound I mostly hear is the abuse of my mother who occasionally answers, but for the most part listens. I am pretending to be asleep as always, but I am rigid and wet with fear and I feel as though I am drowning under the winter coats. Although this happened thirty years ago, I have relived it and many other related experiences hundreds of times.

My relationship with my father was always difficult. It was very difficult to understand or get to know him because he seemed to me at that time to have two sides to his personality: the quick-tempered man of the morning and the more cheerful man in the evening, but argumentative with drink.

This inevitably meant that there was significant tension at home. We always seemed to be waiting for the knock on the door, always at irregular times. He never used his key as he had a bicycle which made it awkward for him. It was always the same though, entry followed by tension, followed by his dinner, and by conversation which, if all was not to his liking, quickly turned to argument and anger.

As a child I thought that the many troubles in our home were unique. I could not fathom that there would be anyone else living under the same cloud that we were at all times. Outside the home my father was gregarious and had many friends. In my innocence I prayed for *quiet*, I prayed that he would die or go away, and promised that when I was sixteen I would beat him up for all he had put us through! At that age I had the feeling of being God-forsaken. How could he let us suffer so? Looking back I find him and see him in my mother's bravery and in my own small courage.

My school work suffered, as I was often like a zombie unable to concentrate as the echoes of my father's voice came back again and again throughout the day. How a parent's words and voice can resound long after they are gone. A memorable exam result was the zero I got in algebra in fifth class. A memorable Saturday lunchtime was when he took me by the back of my neck and told me that I was *nothing*. This was because, at twelve years old, I had dared to criticise him for coming home drunk in the middle of the day. Looking back I was in a constant state of shame. However, I feel now that God's presence was there in my sense of injustice, and again in the courage I found to confront him.

The world was turned upside down one evening when I was about sixteen years old. I came home and my father was sitting in the living room with my mother and sisters. He had been drinking and was becoming increasingly sarcastic. I asked him a number of times to stop and, when it became unbearable, I found myself pinning my father to the wall, shouting at him to stop. I could feel his heart pounding, I could feel his fear, and then I knew that the world had finally turned. I let him go and he walked, shaken, from the room. I didn't beat him up as I had promised myself many years before and

I know now that, strangely enough, this was because I loved him in spite of his ways. Once again, the light of God's presence was there.

He seemed to shrink in later years and as he got older it seemed strange that this man could have been so terrifying and formidable. I never got close to him in the end but I did have more of an insight into him and why he was the way he was. He was insecure and unsure of himself and out of touch with his real self.

He was a heavy smoker and in his early seventies had problems with blood clots in his legs. He was hospitalised many times in his last year, frequently for weeks at a time. When I visited him at the hospital we would get through the first few minutes with distant civility and then settle into an uneasy silence until finally I would say goodbye and make my exit. I wanted so much to be able to talk to him. I would plan before I went in that at least I would tell him about my 'day'. I thought that this would not be too difficult, but when I arrived at the hospital I would be unable to tell him anything about my work. I asked him about his pain and his medication, always the same questions, and he would ask me the usual questions about the children. Occasionally his eyes would light up and he'd make a joke about my being a 'professor'; this made me even more uncomfortable. I wanted to say so much to him and I often wondered if he wanted to say anything to me or my brother and sisters; he was probably unable.

He died on Christmas Eve 1993, probably of a blood clot. The nurse pulled back the screen and there he was, dead. I was surprised at how calmly I took in the scene. At the time I convinced myself that I felt nothing. My sisters wept and we said a few prayers over him and then we left to hear what the doctors had to say about his end. There was some doubt as to the actual cause and they requested that we allow an autopsy, which I refused. I wonder why? He had brought me to a football match when I was very small and he fell while kicking the ball back on to the pitch, causing the players to laugh. I didn't understand and I rushed on to the pitch in front of him to protect him. In death he could not protect himself. I keep asking where is God in my relationship with my father, and I learn that it is here.

Christmas was a strange affair after that. We went about our business over the next few days with stoicism and we enjoyed ourselves when we could. This first Christmas without him didn't seem right. I missed him holding his glass up to me for a whisky refill and the atmosphere was strangely sterile without him. There was no tension but there was an unfamiliar dullness.

In the ten years up until his death, I had become a workaholic, obsessed with my work and all the time taking on extra responsibilities. When there was an extra mile to go I would go three, metaphorically speaking. Weekends, late into the night, no time was sacred, I would work and study endlessly. I needed to be busy. There is a peculiar emptiness in the lives of the *busy*. Often, we are the last to notice it. I had to be busy and preoccupied at all costs. I now know that I had a deep discomfort and an irrational shame about myself. Was I blaming myself for not understanding my father and for not being able to communicate with him?

Six months ago, I began to have severe headaches. These continued day after day and the pain was intense. I continued to work and lecture as I had many responsibilities, not least, hosting an international computer science conference. After seven antibiotics the pain had not dissipated, and I feared that I might have some sort of a breakdown. I could not sleep and was barely coping from day to day.

One night, when I managed to sleep, I had a dream about my father. I don't remember very much about it except that after the dream I felt that I had forgiven him. After this, I experienced a significant emotional release as I was able to express feelings that I thought were never there or were long dead. A friend advised me to have a Mass said for my father. My faith at this time was threadbare as is the faith of many people in the modern world. However, I thought that it made sense so I visited a priest and arranged to have the Mass said in our home.

I felt it strange sitting before the priest, two people in a sense from different worlds, religion and science. I felt a sense of guilt that I was wasting his time with my story but he listened in a way that few people listen and he helped me greatly on that first evening as he has on many evenings since. He gave me cassettes and many readings, including Light out of Darkness, and he agreed to say the Mass.

My prayer life began to revive, although I wasn't prepared for the effort it would take and continues to take, and my own resistance to it. I wanted more than anything to have a true sense of God's presence. I wanted verification. I was impatient and faltered. Why wasn't he listening to me? The headaches didn't seem to be improving. I had great difficulty with the idea that God loved me at all. Sometimes we can *force* our searching and blind ourselves to what is simply before our eyes.

Gradually, over time and with patience, with which

I am not greatly endowed, I am coming to terms with my own darkness. Just as my father had his darkness so too have I. I continue to struggle against busyness and selfishness. I am coming to terms with the physical and emotional pain and the past. I think of them now as storms that blew me, one of the weak seeds, out of the thorns and towards more fertile ground. If we look we can find God in the hard and bitter agony of our trials. He is with us, all else passes.

I think that the dream in which I forgave my father was important. I was feeling guilty. I felt that as the eldest son, I should have been able to put things right. I can now see that the restraint I practised at times and the courage I showed at other times was God's way of supporting me when I seemed alone. Recognising his presence and support encourages me to seek him in prayer, people and events, to thank him when things go right and to trust him when I seem lost or disheartened. Letting go my guilt and my relationship with my father has taught me that I want to come close to God. The Holy Spirit helps me to deal with guilt, to be free and I look forward to a more Spirit-filled future!

A MISCARRIAGE OF LOVE

Frances Molloy

Frances Molloy was born on Rathlin Island, Ireland, and now lives in Warwickshire with her husband and two sons. She is a member of the local hospital lay visiting team and also co-leads Light out of Darkness retreats and parish programmes. She is employed part-time as spiritual care adviser with the national charity, Christian Council on Ageing.

This is a wonderful testimony to the power of a living faith which surmounts and wins through problems, despite medical evidence that was presented. A threatened miscarriage for any loving mother is obviously a traumatic experience; when modern technology contradicts the repeated statement of the GP about the reality of pregnancy, the confusion and pain is even greater. Through still more darkness, light eventually shone and Frances could write: 'I was learning to die to self and live for God.'

K.O'S.

As I came to the close of a Light out of Darkness retreat, the words 'miscarriage of love' were sown in my heart. What did they mean? When I arrived home, a letter was waiting, inviting me to share a life-experience which had touched me deeply. I felt the Lord wanted me to share how a miscarriage had changed my life from a comfortable understanding of God to sharing my whole life with him.

In January 1989 when I was training as a leader with Light out of Darkness, focusing on the human and spiritual growth in our daily living, little did I contemplate the significance of this programme for me. Without it I would not have coped with the mysterious event that followed. It taught me how to be open and truthful before God, who was open to me and concerned for me.

Later that January I sensed I was pregnant. A urine test later confirmed this and all was well. I drew life from the story of the Annunciation and how Mary must have felt in those early months with her child. The gift of love in the womb opened me up to the mystery of God's love. It's natural for mothers to think about names even in this early stage of pregnancy and I felt drawn to naming our child Mary Elizabeth. I had two boys, and deep down I'd hoped for a girl.

I began to feel unwell and so I rested. At one point during my prayers I felt guided to pray Ephesians 3:14–18, that this little child would come to know the fullness of God's love. She was nourished on the Eucharist each day through me. I never thought of this before. It was beautiful contemplating life within life and the growth and formation of humanity. I would talk to God about this and ask him if he loved only those who had two legs, two eyes, etc., or did he love everyone. Even this little child in its formation was loved. I came to understand that eternal life is not given by age or size but by its existence in him.

In early April I was still feeling unwell and contacted my GP who arranged a scan for the following week. A further urine test was given; again this was positive.

Undergoing the scan and waiting for the results seemed like hours. I was feeling tense when the consultant came in and informed me, 'There is no pregnancy.' I couldn't believe it. Fear and shock left me speechless. The consultant suggested hospital admission there and then to remove any remaining tissue from the womb. I knew I felt pregnant and didn't understand why, if there was no pregnancy, I needed to have my womb cleaned out. I found this difficult to accept and asked for time to come to terms with the devastating news. I was advised to return in seven days.

As I was walking out of the clinic that day in a state of disbelief, feeling numb, time stood still. Journeying home, the words 'there is no pregnancy' echoed in my mind, I didn't want to hear them. I couldn't think clearly, I was anxious for our children who were eight and five years old – they would be heartbroken. I had to be strong for them until my husband came home from work. I knew that the Lord was with me.

I realised after a few days that my body hormones had ceased. The baby had died. We told the children the baby was not well, and prayed for her each day. Gradually they realised that she might die and so telling them was made easier. Feeling their pain, loss and disappointment added to my own. I had a relationship with her, which the children or their father had not. I wasn't angry with God.

The fact was that I loved him even more! I knew him as never before. He was there all the time, the long hours of the day, the restless lonely hours of night. I was learning a whole new meaning to 'love through suffering'.

When I returned to hospital on 4 May I was informed there was no foetus, only the placenta had developed. I was relieved. Would anyone have understood my need for a funeral? I thought I was at peace until I heard the doctor confirming space with the theatre for a 'missed abortion'. Only God understood how those words pierced my heart.

Weeks after, my health was still fragile and I put it down to grief. There were no counsellors so in my need I asked the Lord. He suffered, he would understand my turmoil. I used to feel afraid of the words 'valley of darkness' (Ps. 23), but that's where I was. The Lord was there too, so I felt comforted. Sometimes I wanted to stay there, but that wasn't healthy. I knew though that the Lord would bring me through to new pastures. I didn't have the energy for anything, other than taking the children to and from school and going to Mass. I wondered if I would ever get well. I was so weak; often my prayer was 'This is my body' and I'd rest in him.

Six weeks later, however, on 11 June I experienced intense back pain, not unlike labour pains. There was an indescribable warmth about it. On my way to school, I called to see my husband, and popped into the toilets; and there gave birth to the child! The surprise, the shock, yet somehow, also a peace filled my whole being as I held this little child about two inches in length (eight to nine weeks' gestation) in the palm of my hand. The words 'Lord you hide from the learned and clever and reveal to mere children' (Matt. 11:25) and 'at last your servant can go in peace now my eyes have seen' (Luke 2:29–30) just flowed. This was overwhelming, this little one in the womb hidden from the eye of the scan and the hand of the surgeon. At last the truth was revealed. Having experienced the pain of losing and also the joy of finding was indeed a special gift. I felt deep compassion for those mothers who never held their child.

My GP provided confirmation of the death which was necessary for the funeral arrangements. Our priests were very supportive, and I recall our parish priest at the requiem mass saying 'miscarriage is a lonely grief'. True indeed, for no one quite knew what to say to me, a grieving mother, or to us as a family. Having Mary Elizabeth laid to rest in the earth – the inscription on the tombstone 'Our little beloved, called by God from the womb' – was indeed a blessing. She was at home in him who created her, as it is written, 'no one can steal from the Father' (John 10:29). It helped us all to name the baby, thus giving her identity within our family as our child and as God's child.

Re-living the events of 1989, especially during the Lent of the next two years, was a source of healing. Journeying with Christ in his Passion, for example, at the sixth station where Veronica meets Jesus and wipes his face, came the realisation that I would never wipe our baby's face. In my own vulnerability I prayed Christ's Passion from the point of view of my own pain as a sharing in his, knowing we would likewise share in the Resurrection. I was learning to die to self and to live for God. I was being taught how to let go self-love and self-interest and to be born and to live more deeply in God. The awareness of Mary Elizabeth once in my womb had revealed to me the meaning of Romans 8:22–3: 'we too groan inwardly as we wait for our bodies to be set free.' I was now the child that was being born, and I felt that my little one Mary Elizabeth, who was 'in God, in Heaven', was helping me!

In January 1993 news of the heartache of another mother's miscarriage prompted me to read through my own journal highlighting the words 'missed abortion'. I wondered what was recorded in my medical records. As this was prior to the 1991 Act, I had no rights to my records. However, I wrote to the consultant expressing my concern with the terminology 'missed abortion'. The consultant replied confirming a modification to my notes from 'abortion' to 'foetal death'. This added to the healing process that was bringing me to more and more life.

In those five years God has taught me that I am his child, and he confirmed this during a desert retreat when I asked him what love really was. In the deep silence that flowed between us then, I experienced how much he loved me. I hadn't expected him to reveal himself to me in my own poverty, my own self. Then I recalled how special Mary Elizabeth was to me, so why could I not accept that I – and each of us – is a special child to the God who created us! He taught me that I too was once a seed in my mother's womb and loved by my mother and by my God. As my child became part of my flesh so too the risen Christ through his Spirit lives deeply within me (Gal. 2:20) – and his life in me will not be miscarried. He will be my light and he will mark out the way I should walk. Life as his child means freedom, freedom to do whatever he asks of me, in his strength.

This reflection is what the Lord gave me in prayer for a remembrance service at our local hospital for those who, like me, had lost little ones. This reveals a little of his infinite Fatherly love.

Remembering

The joy . . . the expectation . . . as I pondered the news
   of this new life.
I thought of the little seed within me . . . growing . . .
the tiny heart . . . little hands . . . tiny feet . . .
a little person . . . so small, yet so alive.
How can a person be so small and yet whole?
The mystery of Life . . . within me . . .

Which day did God make the fingernails grow?
Which day the eyelashes . . . which day the toes?
All this work going on within the silence of my
   womb.
Which day did God join the nerve to the mouth to
   create a smile?
The mystery of life . . . the joys . . . expectations . . .
   the fears . . .
The fears to become reality . . . dreams shattered . . .
   plans changed . . .
Why God? Why?

LIVING WITH THE GIFT OF DYING

Mary O'Sullivan

Mary O'Sullivan is married with four children and lives in Cork. She has been actively involved in Church ministries since 1972, and is a very dynamic co-ordinator and leader of Light out of Darkness programmes in her area.

An unusual and inspiring story of a woman who continues to live and serve positively with the certainty of impending death as a constant companion. There is a real zest for living here overflowing in joy and yet a convincing realism. 'I believe firmly that if ever I cannot work and spread his message because of ill-health, I can always love him and love everyone else without exception. That is a huge leap in faith for one like me . . .'

K.O'S.

In the summer of 1990 I was invited by the Capuchin Fathers to train in a Way of Life programme, forerunner of Light out of Darkness. That was a week to remember.

For the first time in my life I could recognise an *exciting new beginning* and that was really good. The group who trained on that retreat and workshop heard about all sorts of wonderful things – and indeed some difficult ones too – that went into living a life. No more for me, the kind of life I had been living up to then – over-dependent on self – but a life safe in the knowledge that each one of us was loved as we were by God. This God loved us – colour, creed or religious denomination made absolutely no difference.

We looked at many aspects of our human and religious lives. We saw the voids in our lives, where really there should be none, and we also saw the gifts and the potential that lay within each one of those gifts, no matter how small. From my point of view, six years later, the gift that seems to be the hinge uniting human and spiritual life is one that seems essential to all gifts. I refer to the gift of *awareness*. You may ask me 'awareness of what?' and I would have to say 'of everything', every single moment and every movement in our lives. I find that a day that I am tuned into 'awareness of God in my life' is a happy day. I can reach out to people in the simplest way, I enjoy the day, and my family certainly knows the difference!

I have a husband and four gown-up children and they live with the fact that I have a severe medical handicap. It cannot be cured so therefore it has to be managed by a lot of people. The mainstay of that management is my husband and family. In 1987 I was told that I had about five years to live. I have a severely distorted aortic aneurysm. The first year of getting used to looking death in the face was very hard and prayer was almost impossible. I was not exactly blaming God for what had gone wrong, but I was totally centred on myself and on the painful possibility of leaving my husband and children behind. There were times in that first year when Billy and I would wake in the night and just ask each other, 'What will we do?' Then this settled down somewhat, thanks to prayers from good friends combined with a lot of tender loving care and attention.

The spiritual acceptance of this trauma happened that week in 1990 at the Way of Life retreat. I really found my Jesus – the one I never knew – and through his grace I have not really lost him since, nor he me. Now, that is not to say that I am always aware, but yes, very often I am. Sometimes it is physically hard to get on with the gift of life that God has given me, but by being aware that, yes, I am loved by God and he does want me, eventually, back home with him in time, like everyone else, then I can deal, in the certainty of his love, with almost everything. I say almost, because there are always times in life when my humanity gets in the way of what I feel. Living with the gift of dying was a totally new idea for me. There are no bouquets due to me for that.

The Lord himself keeps the reality before me, and I have to try to be aware enough each day to realise that I have to die to myself and live for God, through whatever channels he sends my way. I would have thought the idea morbid before the retreat in 1990. Now, I see it as the only way I can live my life, a way of mutual loving – God and I. It is a concept that has evolved, much of it, through working with Light out of Darkness, which is the development of the original Way of Life. It has also been made clearer by recognising the fact that there is nothing that we can do to change the path that God has mapped out for each one of us. Nothing, yet everything.

We can learn to say 'Yes' with Jesus to the Father as Jesus learnt. He has given us this wonderful gift of awareness and through it we can try to be always ready for whatever comes our way – the good and the not so good.

On that particular week in 1990, I knew something had happened and I felt fired with a great sense of urgency. Looking back on it I think I went off in all directions at once! I thought that was it and it would end there, but no, each day reveals more of God's love and forgiveness to me. So, life has become far less complicated and much more deeply joyful. It is as if Jesus and I had a secret and I really am not able to put the effects of that into words! Life has changed many times and I have been through many different and rough phases, but God is always there – the centre of my life. I can relate to him, tune in to him as it were, through Jesus, and then all is well.

What have I done about this programme which I experienced in 1990 and which affected me deeply? As you know, if you hit on any new good idea, there are always people who are willing to listen. So as I thought this was a life-changing idea, for the better, I started working with like-minded people who had also trained in the course. The initial idea has now been transformed into Light out of Darkness programmes. There are at any given time in our area in Cork six groups of ten to twelve people systematically going through the course with the accompanying book, each group being helped by two of our trained leaders. The same is happening in Dublin, Donegal, Waterford – wherever people are willing to be set on fire.

So now, at fifty-two years of age, and nine years on from when we were told that I had about five years to live, I have to believe that no matter what way I conduct my life, God is always near and ready to help if I but ask. Prior to 1990 I would have asked friends and professional people to help me cope with this ill-health which limited my life in imperceivable ways. Now, I ask God because I know he is aware of what is truly going on in my life, and most importantly what my attitude to it is at the time. He has never failed me.

I would love to finish off my story by saying that I feel that I am well on the way to sainthood, but no, what I feel is that I am beginning to believe and trust, and that is great. When I now say, now, that I believe, I really mean it, and when I do not believe I feel lost until God comes to find me again. I believe now that when God gives us a gift, he wants us to use it for other people and so it spreads and God delights all the more in who we are and in what we are doing for him. I believe firmly that if ever I cannot work and spread his message because of ill-health, I can always love him and love everyone else without exception. That is a huge leap in faith for one like me who always thinks that to be of any use you must be doing – something – like Martha, but now I know that nothing is impossible with God. I have learnt that he delights in us whenever we praise, glorify and thank him. It takes a moment – a treasured moment – of joining the whole court of heaven to rejoice in the wonder of our loving and invincible God.

FROM DEATH TO LIFE

Christine Hillman

Christine Hillman is an accredited Christian counsellor and psychotherapist working in private practice. She is also a trustee and part of the management team of the Crowhurst Home of Healing in Sussex. Although now an active member in her Anglican church, she has been greatly influenced by her time with the Quakers.

Despite the negative findings of paediatricians and neurologists with their clear, unequivocal message to the parents of an infant whose brain was severely damaged – he has 'no capacity to develop' and will probably die at eighteen months – the mother, Christine, turned to God. The quality of faith that emerges in this testimony is strong, rooted in Christ, full of courage, lit with an eagerness to share with others the wonder of a God who not only heals, but transforms lives – because he loves.

K.O'S.

At the time when our second son was born, Christian faith for me was about worshipping a distant and demanding God.

Our baby, whose arrival had been joyfully anticipated, was severely brain injured shortly after his birth. 'Sadly he's severely mentally retarded with no capacity to develop; his reflexes aren't functioning, he can't feed; put him in a home and get on with your life; he'll probably die of a chest infection when he's eighteen months old.' These were the statements made to us by the consultant paediatricians and neurologists.

I was numb, shocked and horrified that absolutely nothing could be done to help him. We couldn't accept 'putting him into a home', but, equally, I struggled profoundly with the idea of bringing him home and keeping him alive when he had no capacity at all to live life as we know it. I remember saying to our Christian doctor that I felt I just couldn't bring him out of hospital without some sort of reassurance that there was hope that he might be able to develop in some way – albeit small. He said he understood how I felt and was sorry that nobody could give any reassurance.

In those circumstances what was there to do other than to turn to God? Man could do nothing. All I knew was that I had to be with God in an open way. I wondered where I could do that. Following a 'hunch' to telephone the Quakers, I later found myself staying for a week in their home of healing which was just a couple of miles from where we lived. Until that time I had not known of its existence or that God healed people. I had realised that that was something Jesus did when he was on earth, but not in the present!

From the time I walked into Claridge House, it felt

as if I was being profoundly supported. A new world seemed to be opening up that I had never encountered before. They told me that the 'celestial civil service' was in action! Hundreds and then thousands of people from all denominations started to pray for us. It just seemed to happen. The Quakers introduced us to an Anglican healing centre, Burrswood, where we received the laying-on-of-hands on Ben's behalf.

It was there, in the chapel courtyard, under the cut-out cross, called the 'breakthrough cross', that I first felt with a profound sense of awe and amazement a power, a flowing energy that I did not understand but knew, without doubt, was coming from God. We continued to visit Ben daily in hospital. His condition was unchanged – he was immobile, unresponsive and tube fed. On calling into Claridge House a week later I was given a book called *Power in Praise* by Merlin A. Carothers. As I started to read it that evening my reaction to its message, as I understood it, was strongly resistant. How could I possibly praise God for the situation my baby was in? That was ridiculous to me. Thank God for a baby with no capacity for life? It seemed a sick joke. But I didn't understand the ways of the Spirit then. All I knew was that I seemed to be gently led to hand over the situation to God, let it go to him, stop trying to sort it out myself – in other words, surrender it.

After a profound inner struggle I committed Ben and his problem to him with as much trust and thanks as I could muster – which wasn't very much. I remember asking God not to ask me to give my life to keep a child alive who had no capacity to live: if he could possibly heal him (as I had learned by then that others had been healed) I would offer my life to work with people in whatever way he desired.

The next day, during a telephone conversation with a relative stranger, I felt that power that I had felt in Burrswood (now understood as the power of the Holy Spirit) flowing through me when she said to me, 'He'll be fine.' I couldn't understand why I had felt that and mentioned it to my husband in the car on the way to the hospital. Amazingly, as I related the experience to him and repeated the words, 'He will be fine', the car was flooded with that power. We both felt it for some time. We knew it wasn't anything we were imagining. It was real, tangible, and we were both convinced that it was from God. We knew for sure that we had been given a promise that Ben would be fine, completely contrary to the reality we recognised very clearly. When we arrived at the hospital Ben seemed to be the same except for one small thing. He squeezed my husband's little finger – the first sign of life we had seen in him. We interpreted that one small squeeze as confirmation of what we both knew; despite all human logic and knowledge, Ben would recover. It seemed that the impossible was possible for God and I remembered with a sense of wonder what I had said to our doctor three weeks earlier, that some kind of reassurance was needed before I could bring him home.

We thought the doctors would think that we were deranged if we told them what we now believed. They were surprised enough that we asked to take him home. As we left the hospital one of them warned the trained nurse who was going to spend the first month of Ben's life at home with us, that she didn't know what she was letting herself in for. Indeed, it was a question of keeping him alive for the first couple of years of his life. Hours were spent pouring milk down his throat from a teaspoon. He wasn't able to suck or even swallow. My faith in God's promise wavered. Had we imagined it after all?

But, no, Ben started beginning to show signs of life. When he was eighteen months old, it felt as if he was here at last. A person was present. He began to practise smiling. First one side of his face would turn up, then the other. The best Mother's Day present I've ever had was when he managed to lift both sides and produced his first smile.

The paediatricians were astounded that he was beginning to do things but also impatient with me that I refused to accept their statements. 'You must accept, Mrs Hillman, that Benjamin will never sit or stand or walk or talk', one consultant said when Ben was three years old. Six months later that same man said he simply had to come to tell me personally that they were all absolutely astounded that Ben was standing in his cot. Even then I didn't have the courage to tell him about God's promise, although I did tell him that I believed that prayer had had much to do with his remarkable progress.

And so Benjamin's recovery has continued. He's twenty years old now and not only does he sit, stand, walk and talk, he's just coming to the end of a course at Agricultural College! He is spiritually very mature, with a great personality and sense of humour. He has just a little further to go for the healing to be complete. He has now taken over from us that trust in God's promise, doing all that he can to help himself and leaving the rest to God, who seems to have used so many channels of healing to bring Ben into the fullness of life he desires for him: the medical profession, the Christian healing ministry, teachers, close family, friends and many more. Christ, the healer, has been incarnated in so many people and situations, evidenced not only in Ben's movement towards wholeness but also in all who have been involved. The 'divine circulation' of the healing love of Christ is touching all of us, moving us all towards the wholeness he desires for each one of us.

Speaking personally this experience has been for me an experience of the cross and the Resurrection at the same time. God's promise about Ben's recovery didn't mean that the grieving process for his loss of ability to live life didn't happen. It did, profoundly. The agony of seeing one's child rejected by people because of his handicap was not lessened. The worry about the effect on his elder brother was still profound. But it was a time of refining; a time when my values were sifted; when God's gift of life was recognised with the reverence and gratitude it deserves; when awareness increased that there's a gift to be discovered in every life experience. The greatest gift, of course, is his presence in it, his saving and healing love offering truth, hope, healing to each one of us according to our need. And we are all invited to share in his redemptive process as we reach out with him to meet others at their point of need, thus being part of his transforming work of bringing light out of darkness.

LURE OF THE SIREN

Tony White

Tony White is a general medical practitioner in Newmarket. He is a member of the Medical Research Council GP research framework and assistant director of studies in the department of general practice at the Clinical Medical School in Cambridge. He is married to a nurse and has two children. He plays an active part in his Anglican parish and helps to organise and lead Light out of Darkness groups.

This testimony traces convincingly – from personal experience – the process of spiritual growth from a relatively innocuous interest in spiritual matters to serious involvement. There is a trigger-point in one's life-experience which alerts the seeker; growth follows, only to be tested eventually, by the lure of the sirens. These pleasing obstacles nourish self-love and distract from God as central to one's life. Particularly helpful is the writer's honesty in sharing his own anxieties, and in describing the sirens which can lure him away from his deepest desire. Emphasis on the need for discernment and guidance is both practical and timely.

K.O'S.

About once a year we hear of a new supertanker disaster. A ship, loaded with crude oil, sailing on a routine journey, anticipating no difficulty, expects to make port in good time. But then, through bad weather, inattention, lack of care, faulty navigation or other human error, disaster suddenly looms. A ship is lost and thousands of tons of oil pollute the environment. Ships with lethal cargoes seem to be lured on to the rocks. It happens so regularly that I think of the sirens. The sirens of Greek mythology lured unwitting sailors to their doom with their beautiful singing. How could something so beautiful be so dangerous?

I have had trouble with the lure of the sirens in my life. Let me explain.

I have no dramatic events to recount, no Damascus road experience, but a lifelong tussle with myself, with God and with the enemy – whom I liken to the mythological sirens.

I was blessed in my childhood with a stable and loving home. I was always an achiever and never found success elusive. I have always been able to do what I really feel called to do – and now feel fulfilled in my work as a doctor. I have been gifted and I am truly grateful. I try to use my gifts to the best of my ability. My upbringing was Christian, both in my home and in my education. Furthermore, I have always had an interest in spiritual matters, although it was a tenuous interest throughout my teens and twenties. In my thirties I made a conscious decision (during a brief illness) to take my faith more seriously, which brought the spiritual blessings of increased faith, hope and love.

A few years later I met Kathleen O'Sullivan when she registered as a patient. Through Way of Life (later Light out of Darkness) I learnt to look at my relationship with myself, with other people and with God in greater depth. All this was completely new to me. About half-way through the course I realised that I was being transformed. I recognised this because for the first time in my life, deep down, I no longer wanted to be someone else. How could I have wanted to be someone else? God was clearly saying, 'You are my special creation. You are who you are intended to be. I do not want you to be different. Come to me as you are. Love me as you are, and let me love you as you are.' What did it mean?

I realised that deep down, I was dissatisfied with myself, and, yes, in some measure envious of others. Slowly, in prayer, and with guidance, I came to realise that what drove me, what made me strive to achieve, was a deep-seated sense of insecurity which I compensated for by means of obsessional drive, ambition, diligence, over-busyness. I recognised in myself what I had so often seen in others. I was driven not by the worthy motives that I imagined. I was driven by a fear of failure. I had to prove to myself that I had worth. I have always been my harshest critic. At the age of eight my headmaster wrote on my school report 'an able lad – a pity he resents criticism'. How much that remark stung me – it stays with me even now – but it stung because it was true.

It was a revelation to me to come to believe, to actually experience, that God really loves me as I am. He loves the 'real' me, not the false me that I present to the world. He loves the sordid, nasty bits of me, which I hide from the world, which I hide from myself, and which I try to hide from him. It is the failings that are truly my salvation – how arrogant and proud I would be if I did not have my recurring failures!

I have whole layers of anxiety, self-concern and insecurity to shed, but I now recognise that this is a process of growth into freedom. This freedom is the freedom to be the real me. Little by little I am learning to understand in my heart, not just in my head, that God is greater than my limitations, that he created me, and that he finds me lovable. With that base, I have a sure foundation from which to grow into the 'real' me, and from which to reflect God's love to the world. I know that I am beginning to lose some of my need to seek approval, love, praise from others (to have my 'ego' fed). I feel less need to make people dependent on me as a means of proving my value to myself. To that extent I am becoming a little less self-centred and a little more Christ-centred.

It all sounds such very Good News, so where is the lure of the siren?

I am a slow learner, and often slip back into old ways. I often find myself seeming to take one step forward and two back. The process I have described is a slow one, not a quick revelation. I need time to be still, time for reflection, time for God to work on me. Once a year, or thereabouts, I have been able to make time for a retreat. Daily, I try to have quiet time with the Lord. But it seems that there is a cycle in which I get caught, of increasing busyness, increasing commitments. These have the deleterious effect of putting my life off balance – squeezing out proper leisure time, time with my wife and family, and time set aside for God. Although each of these commitments seems to be the right thing to do, the cumulative effect is devastating.

Excessive busyness protects me from the need to look at myself, from looking deeply into the mirror, and it deludes me into thinking that I am working for God when in truth it is the snare of the enemy – the lure of the siren. The over-commitment, even to things that are in themselves worthy, is a trap. It leads me from freedom to bondage, from light back in to darkness.

In my foolish pride, I imagined that I had learned that lesson, but recent events have proved me wrong. Again I have heard the sirens' song and headed for the rocks, tired and heading for 'burn-out'. This time God is calling me back from the edge of disaster, and back out to safer deep water. Several reasons prevent disaster: I have learned some discernment, I had some guidance, and I was able to recognise that I was on the wrong course. I have also learned that the devil is truly the great deceiver, the 'angel of light', who is most dangerous and most cunning when we are most earnestly seeking God. How could it be otherwise? Not much work for him to do when we are far from God!

This sharp lesson, painful and difficult to learn, reminds me that there are layers of uncertainty, layers of insecurity in me, still to be revealed. And each layer of insecurity, leads to a choice: to let go of my need for a 'security blanket' and grow into a more mature, free, real, Christ-centred person, or to cling to my security and remain relatively retarded. It is a plain enough choice – 'choose life or choose death' (Deut. 30). In my insecurity I use the mechanisms of being too busy, too active, to block out the basic dissatisfaction with the self-centred me.

It is difficult to be more Christ-centred and less self-centred, but I deeply desire to follow this course. It must be a minute by minute business, trying to be focused on Christ, only concerned about this moment. It comes down to being totally real, and thinking only of the now. All else is futile.

I believe that in the mythological story, the sirens' song was perceived differently by different sailors, each hearing it as the most attractive thing he could imagine. Such is the deceiving spirit, the false angel of light, Satan. How can I detect the action of the enemy? I must continually discern whether activities are leading me towards God or away. I must read the warning signs of irritability, excessive and unexplained tiredness, depression. However worthy or 'good' my activities seem, if they detract from my relationship with God, I must look carefully at what I am doing. Recognising the truth about my situation will set me free. Deception, above all self-deception, leads to bondage, to ensnaring, to a collision course with the rocks.

Therefore, I must beware the lure of the siren, but I no longer have so much fear, because I have experienced the Lord's hand reaching out to rescue me.

HOPE

'Hope that is seen is no hope at all . . . but if we hope for what we do not yet have, we wait for it patiently' (Rom. 8:24–5).

'We fix our eyes not on what is seen, but on what is unseen. For what is seen is temporary, but what is unseen is eternal' (2 Cor. 4:18).

When we are filled with hope which, as already, said, is accompanied by faith and love, then we are filled with the energy of the Spirit to allow ourselves to be used by God in the fulfilment of his plans for the kingdom.

As God's plan for each unfolds, then faith or love or hope shines out according to the need of the moment and our inner response.

A particular aspect of hope seems to be 'surrender and commitment', because we have come to know – in and through hope – him whom our soul loves and to whom we entrust all that we are.

LET HIM

Barbara Brosnan

Barbara Brosnan is a linguist, a trained nurse, a qualified physician. She was a doctor in a Bristol hospital from 1953 to 1961 and then she opened a house for physically handicapped people of all ages and all degrees of disability.

The clarity of vision and the sense of humour of our eighty-year old, I find a delight – giving new hope to all of us who are willing to drink deep of her wisdom. The treasure of spirituality that underlies every thought cannot be absorbed at one reading. At eighty, Barbara is still on call 'twenty-four hours a day' to all who call, but she is indeed 'letting him'. God surely loves her as we do!

K.O'S.

It was a very ordinary confession – impatience once or twice; irritability; lack of charity, both in thought and word; inattention at prayer and Mass; instances of selfishness. I had often made similar confessions. But

151

the penance was not ordinary. 'Barbara', he said, 'there is only one penance I can give you – just two words – "let him"'.

'Let him?' I queried. 'Yes, just "let Him".' Nonplussed, I pigeon-holed the penance for later consideration, made an act of contrition, received absolution and departed.

Later that same day as I carefully surveyed that same penance, I liked what I saw less and less. Let him? How? When? What did he mean anyway? At first perplexed, I quickly became first irritated, then angry. I had only met this Canadian priest recently. Known as the 'singing friar' in the sixties, he had become a very sick man following an horrific car crash, but had acquired a reputation for uncanny insight.

The following morning, still indignant, I returned, having brooded over 'let him' all night.

'That penance – how could you?' I burst out. 'I shall never be free of it – it will just go on for ever!'

'I know', was the reply.

'But – how could you give me something so impossible?'

'Barbara, I had to.'

End of conversation.

I was seventy then, now I'm eighty. I wish I could say that from that moment on I was a different person, but it would just not be true. What is true though is that it changed the whole pattern of my life.

I was struck first of all by my own reaction – the absolute acceptance that what he had said was relevant, and would prove both difficult and time-consuming. No instinctive response that I did 'let him' anyway. But I would have claimed to have given my life into his hands years before. There was something wrong somewhere.

How then did I live out this gift of self to God? It took me several days to work that out. Then I realised that I was confident that I knew his will and I had taken over. It was not: 'Yes, Lord. I see this is your will – show me how it is to be done – the work is all yours.' Everything had become doing *my* will not *his* and being in control myself. I was too sure of myself to listen to the voice of God before launching into action, and saw everything through my own eyes. *I* knew the person God intended me to be, knew the work he wanted me to do in his service. Always I. I. I the planner, the organiser, the do-gooder, serving him my way, totally convinced that it was his way. All these complacent years my fundamental attitude had been wrong. And try to change that at seventy!

I couldn't but he could. His timing was exact and the path he mapped out perfect. Was he not God?

Just before I made that confession, I had decided that much as I loved my work, it was time to retire or there might be no time left for living after retirement. However absorbing the job, seventy was late enough.

I was running a home for forty-two severely physically handicapped people of all ages – sixteen to ninety plus – with a staff of seventy and more than a hundred voluntary helpers. Although a nursing home where residents could stay until death, there was every type of activity – basic education, music, drama, art, cookery, yoga, needlework, computer literacy, riding, swimming, holidays (camping and abroad). A Christian home, the chapel had an important part to play. I had started the home and run it for nearly twenty-five years. Being the resident doctor, I was on call twenty-four hours a day, seven days a week, and every death was like that of a relative or close friend. We were one enormous loving family where everyone was of equal importance, staff and residents alike.

I gave a great deal of thought to my strange penance. Clearly, God himself would have to teach me how to stop trying to be always in control, and instead to 'let him'. My problem was – where was the 'real' me for him to teach? This real person had, I felt, become submerged beneath an enormous volume of work and a routine of rushed spiritual observances. Yet I knew that, somewhere, though lost, there must be that real 'me' whom God loved, but who had become buried over the years beneath good works and pious practices. Now I had to stand totally surrendered, totally transparent before the God I felt genuinely called upon to follow. Then, and only then, could his will really be done. And while he had been longing to give himself to me, I had been ever so busy being good and doing good to my own satisfaction. What I had actually succeeded in doing was to create an unreal me and an imaginary God! 'Letting him' would necessitate a different way of life altogether. It would be like saying 'Fiat' with our Lady.

Once retired, I spent six weeks in a Christian ashram in India. I only came out of my hut twice a day – once at 5 a.m. for meditation, office and Mass and again at 4 p.m. for tea and the only conversation of the day. Otherwise my time was spent in silent solitude. I had no books; I knew they could too easily enable me to put off facing God himself in prayer. It was a scant six weeks, but time enough for some of the unrealities, the cover-up masks to shrivel somewhat. Silence, solitude and God – to the exclusion of all else – have this effect. The God you encounter in prayer this way breaks down your defences, forcing you to see yourself as you really are and this is painful. Encounter with God is not always a pleasant, soothing experience; it can be brutally surgical at first. Yet this surgery brought about that silence in my heart without which the voice of Christ is not heard.

Back in England I was now a voluntary worker in the home myself. This I greatly enjoyed at first but after a year or so things began to change. More and more staff were taken on – 'the state will pay' – and voluntaries quietly sidelined as unnecessary. We were told that fund raising was now not needed – we used to raise in excess of £12,000 a year – and anyway staff could do all that the voluntaries had done. There was no longer the aim of developing each individual resident to their full potential physically, mentally and spiritually. A Christian ethos seemed no longer to exist and the home was rapidly becoming an institution where loving service had been replaced by just getting the job done. Actually it closed within three years through not being financially viable, but it had died well before.

I was saddened, but work for God has value only for as long as he wants it and his ways are inscrutable. It was not difficult to accept the closure. What was more difficult to accept was the hurt and bewilderment of so many people forced to move elsewhere. But the joy, happiness and comradeship that the house had brought into being was indestructible. So many residents had lived out their lives surrounded by love and had died in peace there. The many friendships forged remained – and do so to this day. I mourned for those who mourned, but without bitterness.

During those three years, I encountered evil as I never had done before. I saw it lurking behind the eyes of ostensibly caring people. But, as I was once told, the

Father holds all the threads of our lives in his hands, so it is pointless to dwell on the Herods, Pilates and Judases that we might encounter. He has his own mysterious purposes. One thing I did learn, however, was the need for continual prayer to the Holy Spirit that the angel of darkness might not, masquerading as an angel of light, entice me into actions that might falsely seem to be in the service of God. This brought me to sitting like a beggar at the feet of God, praying to receive the gifts of the Spirit, praying that I might long for God himself and not the things of God. 'Let him' was always in my mind and heart.

His timing, again, was perfect. After those three years, never having been really ill, I found myself having three operations in quick succession! A straightforward hip replacement was followed a year later by an exceptionally painful pioneering but successful operation on the knee. Then came major surgery for cancer with accompanying fierce chemotherapy. This last stripped all unrealities away – there was neither time nor energy for disguise. Somehow all experience can bring us closer to our own inner reality if we persevere on our pathway towards him.

In short, having cancer brought me closer and closer to God – there was no escape from 'letting him'. I became more and more aware of his ever loving tenderness. I felt myself hammocked in the love and prayers of those around me, supported and unafraid. Knowing that he is all love, and can only act in love, I felt totally safe. There was time for prayer but in the monotonous desert of having chemotherapy it became a very different prayer. It was really an attitude of prayer, a longing to be praying. Everything was suddenly so simple – which is not the same as being easy. I had always produced complications for myself by getting in my own light, being unreal. Hindrances are in ourselves not God.

So where am I now? From the vantage point of eighty, I see that in his loving kindness he sent or allowed those events and circumstances guaranteed to bring about in me such changes as were necessary if I were ever to be able to 'let him'. There are still loose strands that reason and intelligence do not seem able to draw together – love alone can do that. Knowing that he is all love and can act only in love warms my heart with an awareness that everything is steadily bringing me closer to the everlasting arms.

Now my sight is not what it was and my (previously super acute) hearing leaves something to be desired. I often find it difficult to remember names but there is a deep abiding joy burning within me like a slow fire. Joy over what? I cannot say. The cause seems nameless.

Where am I then? Certainly I have not got very far, but the travelling in his hands has been good. I no longer expect to know what is going on. I have no preconceptions, no programmes for myself, no solutions to the problems of the world. I simply know that at best I see a shadow of the truth. And, yes, I shall never be shut of my penance; yes, it will be with me for all the days he allows me. Comprehension and planning decrease, only love increases. My prayer is not a matter of hours of time but of a retreat into God from which I return to the midstream of living. The intention of praying remains with me always so I know the heart is praying. I can laugh with the Spirit, rejoice with the Lord, cling to the Father – and love, love, love the one, the infinite. But not all the time. Mostly I just get on with the simple things that life is all about – the shopping, preparing the vegetables, doing the dusting, watering the garden, ferrying people to and fro in the car, helping people a bit by writing, 'phoning or visiting. It is all his work; I just try to 'let him'.

LISTENING TO GOD'S CALL – THE MARRIED WAY

Monica O'Reilly

Monica O'Reilly lives in Monkstown, Co. Dublin. She is married to Tommy and has four children. Monica is a past president of the local St Vincent de Paul Conference which addresses the needs of lonely and marginalised people, and in 1988 she was involved in setting up a resource centre in a nearby local authority housing area in an attempt to help people to help themselves. She also leads Light out of Darkness programmes.

For Monica and her husband Tommy, the experience of marriage as 'sacrament' is what has worked. The writer says 'it is not soft or easy'; it requires from all – parents and family – 'a dying to self, so that we can be a channel of God's love anywhere in the world'. Despite life's inevitable storm clouds, joy, gratitude, love, faith, hope and peace of heart flow to the reader. It has much to say to the pre-marital and married world.

K.O'S.

I have been married to Tommy for twenty-four years and our marriage has been graced and blessed with four special children. In our home, six people are managing to live out their individual lives together. Nowadays, as many institutions are collapsing, people are voicing reservations about the institution of marriage also. The question arises in my mind as to how any marriage can survive when the structures surrounding it no longer seem to be holding. It has often amazed me how a marriage of two individuals, from different backgrounds and varying life-experiences, can endure the vicissitudes of modern living and last a lifetime together. This is especially amazing when one considers the arrival into this marriage of children with their own individual needs and different personalities – to say nothing of their hopes and dreams! My own experience of marriage as 'sacrament' has helped me to understand how it is that marriages do survive and can flourish.

The key to this understanding for me is faith in a faithful God. My own childhood experience was of growing up in a large family. My parents placed great emphasis on the practice of their religion. God was 'outside' and was somewhat to be feared but I understood that this God was also faithful. My human experience of a lot of loving within the family opened me to the reality later on of a loving personal God. Very early in my life I often retreated to a 'God space' where I knew that I would be heard and understood. I experienced God as close to me in my precious 'alone' times – which in hindsight I now call prayer time.

I heard God's call to the *married way* almost twenty-five years ago. The initial call was important and strong enough for Tommy and me to make a choice about each other and about this way of life. I believed that it was God's plan that I should marry Tommy as we vowed to be with each other in a special Christian married way. We had faith in each other to believe that we could accept all the tribulations and joys of marriage until we parted at death. My faith now has expanded to recognising both of us together held 'in God', who has been our 'rock and refuge' throughout. As I look back now at all that has happened during those years, I notice with awe how God has been directing our lives. The words of the prophet Hosea resound with me: 'He has led me with reins of kindness and leading strings of love' (Hos. 11.3).

The discovery that I am in relationship with a personal God of love was a turning point in my life. My blindness about this special love relationship between me and my Creator was due to *unawareness* about so many other realities, especially relationships. That blindness was blocking not only my own growth but also the development of my close relationships. Gradually I began to experience what 'living life to the full' really meant. In the early days of our marriage, we really believed that 'having it all together' was the recipe for a happy marriage. Consequently, being financially secure and being in control of our lives and our children were the goals to be achieved. At a mid-point in my life, however, God caught me in 'the unconscious places of my heart' as Patrick Kavanagh so perfectly expresses it.

Through Light out of Darkness, I became aware of God's presence in all the events and encounters of my life. I discovered how closely almighty God was holding me in his care. I realised that he was also deeply concerned about those people he had given to me, whom I could help and with whose help I would develop. Consequently, all my relationships and my whole life began to take on new and deeper dimensions. Being freed from over-concern about my own family – because of an exceptional husband – I discovered needs around me and was free to minister both in the parish and eventually further afield. I experienced being turned upside-down through my involvement in the St Vincent de Paul Conference in our parish. I was having considerable difficulty reconciling our privileged lifestyle and the contrasting lack of privilege of some families in our parish. The ideal of charity or real Christian loving became, insistently, something which had to be 'incarnated' in me if I were to become an authentic follower of Christ. I felt a new call to become more and more real in Christ, for Christ and for all his people. But it had to begin in myself and in my home!

As a parent, I used to feel that it was my responsibility to teach my young children everything, to be responsible for everything they did and to control everything about their lives. All of this with the noblest of egotistical intentions! As they entered the 'turbulent teens', I began to see the uselessness of my striving. My efforts to control them often ended in a battle for control. Ultimately (and fortunately) I discovered that, without their being aware of it, they could be and often were my teachers if I listened deeply to God! More importantly, however, I made the amazing discovery that my children are sacraments of God's great love for me! This requires deep reflection and also being 'taught by God' in prayer and in life. In little ways, I can value and appreciate their surprise manifestations of goodness, kindness and support of other family members. That I am able to grow in God's love through my children casts a new light on my perceptions of parenting! We receive as well as give to one another.

Recently a friend invited me to a play by Sebastian Barry called *The Steward of Christendom*. At one point in the play, the main character describes the moment after the birth of his daughter when he held her in his arms for the first time. He describes the moment when he saw, among the folds of linen, the smallest face he had ever seen. Something very powerful happened to him then. The eyes seemed to be looking directly into his eyes. He said that God showed him at that moment that he would invest all his loving and all his future in that small face. It was a moment of truth – seeing his child as sacrament. It reminded me of the births of my own children and my examination of each of those precious small faces as they arrived in our world. I know something of the huge investment of time and loving in our children. When I notice, however, God's investment of trust in us as parents, it evokes a response. The response is to love these children unconditionally. They are not mere possessions, but are unique human beings who are ours because of our marital love in God. Their destiny is to grow into the image and likeness of God. I find it extremely challenging that my handling of them can either block or encourage that growth.

Through the years, as Tommy and I grew and changed, as circumstances changed, and as we welcomed our four precious children into our marriage, we have been recalled again and again to the commitment of our marriage vows. Tommy's quiet, patient, constant, loving of me and of our children has been a sign of God in my life, a sacramental sign! Through my husband, I have encountered something of the love, the constancy and generosity of our mysterious and wonderful God. I recognise how we have been generously blessed by the grace of God throughout our marriage. This grace which I believed we would receive within the sacrament of our marriage has been on so many occasions the 'glue' which has bonded us and the 'oil' which has freed us. I imagine grace as a most wonderful, fragrant, pure oil which is flowing freely in our marriage. It lubricates all the rusty, malfunctioning, near decaying bits which can creep unnoticed into our relationship and also into the relationship with our children. I am dismayed that I can often take almighty God's grace for granted. But although my awareness is sometimes lacking, I am at other times taken by surprise when grace unlocks a situation which has become stuck or when it gently eases a burden. It may be as simple as a smile shared, or an embrace, or a word of encouragement received.

I have discovered that the call to married love is not soft or easy. It involves my husband, my children and myself. It requires from all of us a lot of dying to self, so that we can be a channel of God's love anywhere in this world. But, here, I am looking at my seeking and finding God in it all. I find it challenging and demanding of my time and myself. In human terms, it often seems impossible. I don't always live up to other peoples' expectations nor do they live up to mine. Hurts and misunderstandings are part and parcel of any relationship. There can also be many unexpected difficulties with children and it is easy to get lost. I need to know that I am not alone. I need to know that Tommy is with me and for me. I need to know that God is with me every step of the way. The image of the good shepherd in St John's gospel is a very comforting one for me. I take courage from hearing that the good shepherd 'brings me out and goes ahead of me'. I need to believe that firmly. There are times when I cannot control the people or the circumstances surrounding me. I can go very far astray from the good shepherd. But when I am praying and paying attention he calls me back. I have also found, to my great surprise, that he calls back also 'one by one' those people I am often concerned about. This may not be always in my time or on my terms. However, when I can love patiently and wait, God has always done the saving.

In our marriage we appreciate that we must be continually listening to each other. We have to keep open to each other and to the children in ways that sometimes demand more than we are able to give. We have come to an awareness that our marriage vocation is a call to a way of loving which we are quite incapable of on our own. The struggle is ongoing but our becoming 'one' in mind and heart and spirit, as well as in body, mirrors for us our invisible union with God.

At home, we light a candle at table, a reminder of God's loving presence with us. Older children, who are perhaps embarrassed by the language of recited prayers, seem comfortable with a short blessing, a prayer of thanks or a shared silence. Thus, in such a simple way, we experience something of the sacred in the midst of the insane busyness of daily living, a communion at our kitchen table. The humility and love of God both astounds and confounds!

FREEDOM THROUGH FORGIVENESS

Jackie Gilsenan

Jackie Gilsenan was born in Newbliss, Co. Monaghan, in 1931. In 1956 he was ordained priest for the diocese of Clogher which straddles the border between the Republic and Northern Ireland. Since then, Jackie has taught at St Michael's College, Enniskillen, been curate in Ballyshannon, rector of St Patrick's Agricultural College, priest in the cathedral parish of Monaghan, in Edernay, Co. Fermanagh, and now in Tydavnet, Co Monaghan. He has worked for the Catholic Marriage Advisory Council.

The humility, sincerity and openness of this priest-writer will surely be a healing revelation to many. It takes courage and commitment to write like this: to assess the planks of the past platform; to come out from behind protective barricades, leaving hurts behind; to refuse to shelter behind anyone, no matter how justified; to stand alone before God and one's neighbour, acknowledging one's limitation of vision but ready to build together and with God. This is greatness; this is genuine spirituality. Would that we all could share it! This is the Church of tomorrow.

K.O'S.

A father loses a son; a wife her husband, murdered in her presence in the Northern Ireland troubles. They recount their stories and their ability to forgive. I listen and admire their strength and courage. To be able to follow Christ so closely is a great gift from God. 'Father, forgive them for they know not what they do', he said. To make allowance for the offenders who kill a family member is heroic forgiveness, Christian love at its best. I admired it in Jesus – I admired it in the people being interviewed on TV. I regularly preached about the importance of forgiveness and the evil of revenge and retaliation. Revenge passes from one generation to another when children are taught not to speak to certain neighbours or family members. If I had been asked if I was a forgiving person, I would have said 'Yes'.

I made a Light out of Darkness retreat in 1994. In my quiet listening to the Lord, I got a surprise when I realised how much damage was being done to my relationship with him by my refusal to forgive. I had been hurt by what I regarded as an attack on my integrity by some people in the parish. Gradually, I discovered that my unhappiness was due to my spite and lack of forgiveness rather than the insinuations made against me. When I came to realise this, due mainly to my sharing with others, a weight was lifted from me and I was given the strength to visit the people I held responsible and, without saying much, to show that I had a change of heart. The Lord had helped me to forgive. I was grateful to him and experienced happiness and freedom to continue working with the people who had hurt me and from whom I had previously severed relationship.

Almost two years later, I was invited to do a desert retreat. I was reluctant but felt privileged to be asked and agreed to go. As the time approached, I was secretly hoping that something would happen to prevent my going. When the time came, I felt like one caught in a trap. When, on my arrival, I discovered that there were only seven people in the group I felt vulnerable. I was used to clergy retreats with forty or fifty people where one merged into the crowd. Here I was with a small group used to faith sharing and I felt out of my depth. That feeling was very real on the first night in the retreat house. My small bedroom felt like a cage compared with my own large airy house. So closed in did I feel that I had to leave the door open and the light on to go to sleep. Finally I was able to put off the light but I kept the door open till morning. By the next night I had got used to my small room but my trapped mentality remained. Gradually, I became aware that the weights pressing down on me were the criticisms and attacks on the Church and the priesthood in Ireland in the past few years. That these attacks were coming from within the Church community and from people in our own country weighed heavily on me. I had been lashing out in all directions at the attackers, squirming under the pain. I had stopped buying some newspapers, wrote to journalists, turned off TV programmes and felt angry and helpless. I was truly 'caged'.

I had spent the forty years of my working life as a priest in the Irish Catholic Church. The general direction of my life was in the service of God's people in whatever position I was placed by my bishop. I was happy in my priesthood. It was a great privilege to be called to be a priest. I was *proud* of my priesthood.

I was sure that my Church was faithful to the teaching of Jesus Christ and was continuing the work of spreading God's kingdom. The Irish Catholic Church had survived persecution and the penal laws and had a strong missionary tradition. I was *proud* of my Church.

Fortunate to be born into a happy family, I still enjoy the love and support of my brothers and sisters, nieces and nephews. The values I inherited from my family served me well. My father had a job good enough to send us all to boarding schools in the 1940s and 1950s, when very few others in our country parish got that chance. My mother used to tell this little story about a neighbouring family when she was young. The young son was overheard saying to his mother, 'Ma, are we quality?' 'No, son,' the mother replied, 'we're not quality but we're a cut above the commonality.' I believe my mother was giving us a message. I was *proud* of my family.

I was born just ten years after independence at a time when there was an atmosphere of hope for Ireland as a young country with a great future, 'a light to the nations'. My parents were involved in the struggle for independence and had the sense of achievement and hope born of newly won freedom. Partition was new and temporary and when removed, we would reach the 'promised land' – Ireland united and Catholic. I was *proud* of my country.

Priesthood, Church, Family, Country. These were the four planks of my platform. Some cracks had appeared in them over my lifetime but it was only in the last two years that the foundations of all I stood for were giving way under me, with the vicious attacks from ordinary Irish women and men. My reaction was twofold. One reaction was to fight and defend; the other was to admit abuse of power in the Church but to see it 'out there' or 'up there'. I blamed it on history, the kind of training we got, the attitude of people to us clergy, the hierarchical nature of the Church. Either reaction left me powerless and frustrated. Caged again. No true freedom.

During the desert retreat, I asked God to let me see myself as he saw me. He showed me an Irish Catholic priest who is very much part of the self-righteous, triumphalist, power-abusing institution which made so many good people angry and which some grew to hate. The *pride* in Priesthood, Country, Church and Family could be summed up simply – *PRIDE* – full stop. I began to see the malaise in my own life, the pride which made me a prisoner. As I began to confront my pride head-on, I felt that this was a manageable battle on home-ground. I was relieved of the worry about the whole world and the Church. The Lord and I would be fully occupied with me. I became resigned and more content and free. A great load had been taken off my shoulders. I thought I was now in the clear but that was wishful thinking!

As time went on, different roads opened up for me like the gradual opening of the border roads around our parish after the cease-fire in Northern Ireland. When, however, the scandals of child abuse came to light and the public perception of the priest was questioned, we had to face the same scrutiny as the perpetrators. We had to endure the same suspicion, the same gossip, the same challenge to prove our worth as persons before people trusted and respected us again. This was a shock. It soon became clear that the problems of the clerical Church in Ireland were much greater than those which were coming to light in the exposures of paedophiles. The anger of the newly educated faithful was released. It was anger at the abuse of power and privilege by the clergy in general over a long time. I couldn't afford to stand aside and criticise the offenders. I had to take my place among the clergy and face the critics honestly. For one who had been proud of being a priest, proud of serving God's people, and who had lived a lifetime in that atmosphere of praise and privilege, this was a great shock. It shook my foundations; it shook my friends. I reminded myself of what Jesus had said: 'If they persecuted me, they will also persecute you.' It was one sign of being his follower. 'They fetched stones to stone him. Jesus said to them, "I have done many good works for you to see – for which of these are you stoning me?"' (John 10:3). I had to learn that we are not innocent victims. I became more conscious of the insidiousness of my pride; my stubborn insistence on getting my own way, certain that it was the right way; my impatience at being contradicted; my anger when my decisions were questioned; my annoyance at being ignored; or told to wait or call at a more suitable time. All revealed to me a lack of humility; a lack of becoming more like Christ. I felt called and challenged by God, the good God of love.

Another road was reopened, the way of forgiveness. Pride and hardness of heart go hand in hand. The hard heart can influence the body language, the tight lips, averted eyes, frozen face, a change of direction and a refusal to meet another. These were not 'big rows' but still enough to hurt my pride and call for the shameful defence of retaliation – maybe only refusing to give a friendly nod, but in my heart it was retaliation all

171

the same. Sometimes I would go on the attack with a sharp tongue just to get even, but really to bolster up my pride. 'The things that come out of the mouth come from the heart and it is these that make a man unclean' (Matt. 15:18).

I am more aware now of being annoyed at slights and contradictions. By coincidence, I have been told a few times in the last six months that I cannot easily take advice and correction or even a suggestion that things are done better elsewhere; that I impose my opinion on other people; that I insist on my proposals at meetings until I get my way. I am conscious of holding spite against people who confronted me or being cool towards people who do not co-operate with me, even holding a grudge against people who do not make their weekly contribution to the church collection! These resentments block and imprison. To be aware of them is the first step. Then comes the softening of the heart and the freedom to act follows on that.

I can only say that I'm grateful to God who has led me out of a darkness which I hadn't seen into the light that is his gift. There is still a long road to travel; but travelling it together, as God's people, who pray together and support one another in compassion and love, recognising that we all need repentance, makes a difference. It makes a great difference for us priests when people accept us as fellow travellers, weak and vulnerable, in need of a helping hand, especially when we humbly acknowledge our need for that help.

Despite the pain of the last few years, I'm happy to say – as are so many of my fellow priests – that we are privileged to be priests of God. We gave him our lives and our best efforts before and now that we are – maybe

– more enlightened, we gladly renew our commitment to God. The best way that those reading this can help us, is to pray with us and for us and for one another. We are all sinners and we are all dependent on the mercy of God. Greater closeness to Christ, our way, our truth and our life, will reveal to us the way to travel, the truth to share and the life he has promised to give us. With St Paul, I say, 'I shall be very happy to make my weaknesses my special boast so that the power of Christ may stay over me' (2 Cor. 12:9).

Tribulation that results in peace and hope can be indeed a blessing in disguise. May I have the courage and strength to receive willingly such a blessing!

CALLED

Perpetua O'Donnell

Perpetua O'Donnell graduated in history and Irish at University College, Dublin, and took an MA in religious studies at Spokane University, Washington, USA. She has taught in Donegal, Ireland and in Montana, USA, and in those sharply contrasting places she has led retreats and parish renewal processes.

Religious life is frequently a mystery to those who are unfamiliar with its depth and true meaning. This writer presents necessary facts: the journey of life – be it as a married person, single, or a Religious – is a blend of sorrow and joy. The important thing is that we have let God's voice resound for us and call us to the particular choice which is part of his plan for us. Commitment is necessary in every walk of life, a commitment to love. Becoming a religious is not a running from the normal human delights which are all God's gifts. In choosing to belong to God alone, one surrenders gladly to him, in love, what one treasures – the joys of begetting one's own family and home.

K.O'S.

I was eight years old when the first stirrings towards Religious life moved within me. My mother had brought me to see the film *Keys of the Kingdom*. This was an uncommon experience for me in my early years but one that I thoroughly enjoyed. My vague recollection of the movie is that an American priest went to somewhere in China and was frustrated at the non-co-operation of a Sister who had been in that mission area before him. I can't remember if they joined forces harmoniously for the good of the mission, but I recall very clearly a deep movement within myself to go to China when I grew up and to be very good to that priest! Time was going to stand still until I could get out there and be an angel of mercy to him! Sounds funny doesn't it? But that deep stirring was very real and was the beginning of a searching and a journey that would finally lead me to enter the congregation of the Sisters of Mercy.

God uses the most ordinary situations and experiences to reveal his plans and designs for our lives. Faithfully, I said three Hail Marys every day after that film (and on the advice of a priest with whom I shared my secret) that I would be a Sister when I grew up. As things turned out, China was closed to missionaries during the Communist take-over and I found myself entering a local Mercy congregation with no missions at that time outside Ireland. 'God's ways are not our ways and God's thoughts are not our thoughts' (Isa. 55:9) was surely true for me when it came to choosing a congregation to enter. My missionary dream faded as my desire to become a Sister grew and the struggle of letting go of my family, friends, teaching profession and fun life became real. Many of my happiest hours had been spent in the dance hall. I loved the céili and ballroom dancing and often during these happy times, thoughts of the 'passing', of the emptiness of it all would come. There must be more to life, something was not being satisfied within me. God was calling me to a life of total commitment to him, for his purposes and in his way. And so in faith and in response I found myself in a Mercy community in October 1959. I had no idea what to expect or what would be involved. I was ready for anything, I thought, and I was unreservedly committing my life to the Lord.

The Noviciate years were a mixture of happiness and pain. I was not prepared for the loneliness of the long summer evenings, the Sunday afternoons and the festive times of family memories. Loneliness was a very real and personal pain and was something I had to share with the Lord, in experience rather than words. Somehow Jesus, who also experienced loneliness, entered into the experience, through his Spirit, and strengthened me to accept the loneliness as part of the journey of commitment to Him. These early experiences of loneliness were to be a great blessing in the apostolate later as I shared the loneliness of others' lives through old age, death, separation and family disappointments. Journeying with these people in understanding and compassion became an experience of God with me, reaching out in love to his needy people and drew me deeper into relationship and dependence on him.

Religious life was full of surprises for me. The joy of sisterly support and love, the sharing of prayer and pain, the excitement of being sent on mission, and the delight in sharing each other's success, these filled my heart with gratitude and helped me rejoice in my calling. But the reality of the human condition, the pettiness and smallness I thought belonged 'outside' were very much part of the daily life and sources of tension and unpeace. Often I found the little crosses of daily living more difficult than the big ones. Wrestling with God in prayer, and dumping all my feelings into his wounded heart, always restored my equilibrium and peace and strengthened me to see beyond the actions of others and move forward in confidence for the challenges ahead. This together with the many occasions of laughter, fun and happiness in community made life worthwhile and personally fulfilling.

Prior to Vatican II, my Religious life was predictable and followed a daily horarium. Any changes, even in times for prayers, were exceptional. Routine, uniformity and conformity were the order of the day. But, surprisingly, Jesus had not called me to a perfect community and told me to love all the Sisters. Rather he had called me to an imperfect one and challenged me to love them all. Responding to the challenge meant taking the pains and pieces of strained relationships, jealousies, pettiness, and rejection to the one who understood all the weaknesses the flesh is heir to because 'he himself was weak' (Heb. 4:15). With compassion and tenderness he empowered me to keep on struggling to love, forgive and accept others as they were and actually to find life in the struggle. He gradually became my refuge, my source of strength, my hiding place, all part of the hundredfold.

The fresh air that Pope John XXIII prayed for during Vatican II blew into a hurricane in Religious life. The call to renewal brought excitement, chaos, confusion and change. Gone were uniformity and conformity. Personal development, Myers-Briggs, Enneagram, seminars, courses, updating, chapters and mission statements flooded Religious life. Routine and regularity were no longer the order of the day. Personal witness and lifestyle were now the 'sign' of the Religious person rather than the dress. Sisters moved to live in flats and apartments apart from the community and traditional apostolates were sometimes replaced by more needed ones.

All these changes opened a Pandora's box of feelings and responses. Some Sisters felt liberated, others challenged; some disappointed, some excited and others frightened and cheated. Where was Religious life going? Was this the end? At the time these questions did not disturb me. All around Sisters were getting involved in justice and peace movements, poverty programmes, environmental issues, women's issues, retreat work, etc. and living committed lives to bring about transformation and make the reign of God happen.

Unexpectedly, I found myself invited to move into parish ministry. I had surrendered my life to Jesus and knew I belonged to him. I had experienced his help and guidance all along the way, so it was with his love, deep compassion and quiet joy that I entered into the messiness, brokenness, joys and pains of the human family. Our God is a gutsy God and enters life in the 'raw'. How petty the problems of Religious life seem in comparison to the crosses of unemployment, old age, alcoholism, broken relationships, child abuse and poverty. As a Sister of Mercy, I am now daily humbled by the experiences of those I serve. Wonderfully and sensitively my life is being blessed and transformed by them. As for judgment images, I praise and thank God for allowing me 'to do it unto him' when I serve others.

When I entered Religious life I knew it was a response in faith. Belonging to a small diocesan group then meant being connected within the Community; not only did we know each other well but we knew each other's family. Community celebrations, jubilees and professions were very special times of liturgy, togetherness and fun. Holidays in groups by the sea were highlights every year. There was a sense of solidarity, of being for each other all along the way.

Now the small diocesan unit has become part of a much larger provincial and national one. While every effort is being made to encourage us to 'connect' within the new realities, we know this will take time and generosity. Big celebrations now take place locally and I have a sense of being 'disconnected' even with the former units. Leadership models have moved from the hierarical to the participative, and local communities are taking on more responsibility for their own life. All these shifts, flows and movements have given rise to many questions and no answers about Religious life as we knew it.

One consequence of all this for me is that now, perhaps for the first time, I 'see' the implication of my faith response. Abraham followed his call 'going he knew not where' and God's promises to him were fulfilled, despite apparent contradictions and suffering. I have a sense now of moving in mystery and of being a pilgrim, while being more inserted than ever in life. The truth of being called to a consecrated life, one of total and radical commitment to Jesus of Nazareth, gives me great energy and peace. I know God has a dream for the human family and that God's dream will unfold through the chaos and the confusion. I do not know what the future of Religious life is but I know who holds the future and the birthing of the new. I rejoice to have experienced the past, to live in the present and to be part of the ongoing journey and discernment.

Leaving everything to follow Christ has been rich with light and darkness, Thabor and Gethsemane, self-fulfillment and self-emptying. With the psalmist 'I committed my fate to Yahweh, I trusted him and he acted' (Ps. 37:5).

For all that was, that is and that will be I praise and thank him.

TO BE A PILGRIM

Linda Stalley

Linda Stalley is an active member of her local Anglican church and the Maranatha Community. She works as a doctor in an inner-city practice and is part of a voluntary medical team for the Barnabas Project for the Homeless in Manchester. She is involved in all areas of the Christian healing ministry, with a special interest in exploring the understanding and experience of the church in the body of Christ.

Here again is courage – of a different kind perhaps: courage as a child to trust Jesus without the usual measure of support; courage to believe in his love-call and to answer with total commitment, while still a teenager; courage throughout to be totally honest, take the appropriate steps, give gloriously of herself as a spendthrift for the sake of the one who is the love of her life; courage to let go past hurts and be most truly the self God created in love.

K.O'S.

'He who would valiant be, 'gainst all disaster . . . his first avowed intent, to be a pilgrim.' The words of the hymn are still as vivid in my mind as the image which accompanied them when I sang as a six-year-old in the school hall at assembly. The thought of fighting for God captured my innocent imagination and, there and then, I resolved to be a pilgrim, whatever that might entail.

Whether God existed was never a question in my mind, it was an obvious fact. The real issue in question was what he wanted of me. What did he want me to do? Where did he want me to go? By the age of seven I was certainly planning to be a missionary, possibly to India, I thought, as everyone else seemed to go to Africa.

Sunday school was the norm in those days, and although I will always be grateful for the loving care of our teachers, the predominant memory was going home when my sister Alison and I were allowed a rare treat from the sweet shop. My parents only came to church once in my recollection – for a 'toy service'. I never could understand why they came on that particular occasion, but Alison and I were keen that the visit was not repeated because my mother's loud singing was such an embarrassment. The embarrassment seemed to be on the other foot, however, when the subject of God arose at home and my spiritual pilgrimage became a walk for two only – God and me.

My book of Bible stories was favourite reading. The only Bible that I had was the Authorised Version and after several attempts to read it – from the beginning of course – I gave up. The story of Samuel was particularly special for me and I often wondered whether God would call me personally in the night. I was ready and waiting, and had already given him my response. He wouldn't have to call me three times! I was eager to do anything that God wanted me to do. A committed tomboy, I was brave and already defended the weak at school. At night, however, the noises in the house and the shadows of the trees outside the window left me rigid with fear in my bed. It was then I discovered prayer. Too frightened even to open my eyes, lest the 'intruder' discover that I was awake, I silently asked God to take away my fear and let me sleep. He never failed me.

Transition to the senior Sunday school brought with it a more modern translation of the New Testament which was a wonderful new discovery, as was the weekly congregational service which we had previously only visited on special occasions. The ensuing discussion group gave me more food for thought. My Christian faith, however, continued to be a very personal and private affair.

At about this time, by virtue of being a Girl Guide, I discovered the local Anglican church and fell in love with the liturgy of the Book of Common Prayer, the ritual of the Eucharist which, for me, had such deep meaning, and the hymns which testified to the love of kindred spirits who had found a way of expressing their innermost thoughts, so close to my own. My announcement to my parents that I was going to be confirmed was more out of duty than out of any desire that they should share in what was for me the outward demonstration of the most important decision of my life. I knew that they could not understand my thoughts and my intentions, just as they questioned my eager attendance at both morning and evening services. I knew, too, that my mother secretly feared the consequences of my Christian commitment, and this unspoken fear became for me a wedge between us.

The following four teenage years were both painful

and exhilarating. My relationship with God became much closer as I discovered more of his nature and his personhood in Jesus. My simple understanding was that I should endeavour to grow more like Christ daily but this brought with it the painful recognition of my immense sinfulness, which in turn became self-loathing. How could I possibly become like Christ whilst I could not fully love my own family? My mother and father had sacrificed so much for my education and my future, but my gratitude was punctuated by tearful anger at their blindness to what was most important to me. I was discovering that my choice to walk with God made me lonely in the world.

I decided very early on that life was to be lived to the full and I entered into everything from sport to schoolwork with great enthusiasm. Commitment to God was also an all or nothing affair and for him I set myself high standards; the goal after all was perfection.

As the time came to make a decision about my future, it was natural for me to ask God what I should do. I sensed within me that his direction for me was quite different to that which I would have chosen, but I gladly stepped out on his path. There was never a question of an alternative route.

Despite failing to achieve one of the grades required for my university place I knew, with a peculiar certainty, that I would be accepted and was soon to find myself alone in my 'cell', the name which seemed to fit most aptly my room in the hall of residence. I knew no one within a radius of 150 miles – the distance from home; my only friend was Jesus.

The following ten weeks were intensely lonely as I was confronted with my inability to make conversation or relate to people in a social setting. I found the course work hard and so busied myself in books and, although this was necessary, I knew I was really using my study as an excuse to avoid people with whom I seemed to have so little in common. Even Sunday worship provided no comfort. The campus service took place in an ordinary room in one of the university buildings, using Series III order of communion which was totally alien to me, and so my feeling of desolation increased. The hardest part to bear was the knowledge that the problem was within me and not others.

The command of Jesus to go out and spread the good news and the exhortations of Paul to join in fellowship with other Christians were like millstones round my neck. The gap between the perfect standards of Christ and my wretched faith grew wider. I was no real use to anyone. I had failed God and my only recourse was to cry out to him in utter desperation. I knew that I could return home without shame and was on the verge of making the telephone call when I stopped and recounted with God the way in which he had so clearly brought me to that place. The God I knew and trusted would not have taken me down one path only to retrace the steps.

But what should I do? To go on in this way was impossible. I laid down my fleece before the Lord. I asked him for a clear confirmation of the direction for my life and the sign should be that someone would show me friendship within twenty-four hours. I didn't have to wait long before there was a knock on my door. A girl, to whom I had barely spoken before, asked if I would come with her to join one of the societies . . . The outcome was immaterial. I had my sign.

From then on it was as if the scriptwriter had changed

in my life. I started to make friends and enjoyed weekly fellowship with other Christians in the hall of residence. The city-centre church which I had previously found too threatening became my regular place of worship. Once again God was taking me on a path which I had not expected but, as before, I knew he was with me and each step brought me closer to him.

Graduation and the transition to earning a living was, for me, a continuum from student days. My life revolved around hospitals and patients and I loved it. My work was a vocation not a job. I observed others, even Christians, become tense and anxious about career moves and CVs, but for me the chessboard, with all its potential moves, was masterminded by the one who had the whole universe in his hands and I had no cause for concern.

Wherever I worked I got on well with patients and staff alike. University friends kept in touch, but I had never known close friendship with anyone other than Jesus and was happy that way. I knew I could trust him totally. He would never let me down. I could talk to him freely about my deepest feelings and I knew that if I remained close to him he would bring me total fulfilment.

As one by one friends got married and started to rear families, the expectation that I should follow suit produced in me intense irritation, especially when my mother suggested that I should be exploring every avenue which might produce a suitable husband. My ready reply was that if God wanted me to be married then he would bring it about, but I knew that deep down I questioned whether I could really be attractive to anyone of the opposite sex at all. I was aware that I had love and goodness within me which was from God and I was able to freely express this at the bedsides of those who were sick, but outside of this role I could not escape from the ugly self-image that had been mine since my teens, a self-image which God in his infinite love and mercy sought patiently to transform over many years.

Another of God's unexpected moves brought me to Manchester, a place where I had never thought of living but but where I discovered the healing ministry of Jesus. Through a community of Christians from all denominations united by the love of Jesus, I discovered a new reality of God's personal love for me, as I am. Through this community of Christians, living their separate lives in their separate homes in far-flung parts of the country, I discovered what it means to belong to the family of God.

And having brought me to the place where I knew that I was loved so immensely by him, God challenged me to love myself, to accept myself there and then as I was, not as I would have liked to be, to love myself as he loved me. And suddenly, for the first time in my life, I found myself willing, even wanting to love and accept myself with all my faults and failings, wanting to love the one whom God had created in love and for love, even myself. The question 'How?' was rapidly overtaken by the simple stretching out of my hands to receive this gift of love which God had been waiting to give for so long. And there was peace. Not the simple peace of security that I had learned to receive as a child, but a new peace, the peace of freedom, the peace of the eagle soaring high in the sky, the peace of unity with all creation, the peace of the freedom to *be*.

The pilgrimage continues, each day bringing new horizons and varying paths underfoot. Each day there is the opportunity to discover more of the constant companion Jesus, who has never left me to walk alone. Now each day brings others who walk the same narrow path, sharing in the exhilaration of the mountain top and the darkness of the valley. The pilgrimage is a path towards wholeness and each day brings healing of past hurts and a deeper love for family and friends.

Now, each day I am discovering who I really am – a single cell in Christ's precious body, his Church worldwide in heaven and earth; a daughter of God our loving Father, whose desire is that all his children are happy; a small branch of the true vine with the capacity to be fruitful; a soldier in the army of God ready to care for the injured in battle.

Now, seeing through a glass darkly, knowing only in part, but walking, climbing, dancing, limping eagerly along the pilgrim way until I see face to face the one who is patiently and lovingly everything to me, and then I shall know fully, even as I am fully known.

Yes, it's good to be a pilgrim.

JESUS – MY LORD AND MENTOR

Dennis Wrigley

Originally trained in architecture, Dennis Wrigley has spent much of his life in senior management in industry. He is a Methodist founder and leader of the Maranatha Community, the interdenominational movement committed to Christian healing, unity and renewal. A writer and broadcaster, he has campaigned on issues concerning children and national standards, and for reconciliation in Northern Ireland.

Dennis is a prophetic figure, larger than life-size in his achievements for God and society, yet humble; self-effacing unless the guns are out; so self-giving until, as happens frequently, one can see only Jesus. This testimony moves me deeply, because knowing this man of prayer and his continuous love for God and neighbour, I have experienced its truth. I owe him a great deal.

K.O'S.

189

I cannot remember a time when I was not aware of the presence of God in the world and in my life.

From early childhood I had a deep sense of his closeness to me and of his love. My initial encounter with him was, I suppose, at the little Methodist chapel where I and my family worshipped each Sunday, and where I felt part of an extended loving family of whom God was, in a very real sense, the Father.

As a young boy I remember walking with my father and grandfather by the sea in a small north Wales town. It was early evening and the lights were shining in the gloom as I silently listened to their conversation about the coming war. I was filled with a sense of sadness and sombre expectation. In due course, as preparations were made for the 'black-out', I had the feeling that in a very real sense the lights were going out and something very evil was encroaching upon Europe and was casting a frightening shadow on my own country. I was aware that a ruthless evil influence was challenging everything which as a young boy I cherished – those things which late in my life I saw to be the very foundations of Christian civilisation.

Even before the war I was aware that vast numbers in Britain had deserted the faith which I as a young boy cherished so deeply. Even at this stage in my life I was aware of the profound spiritual nature of the conflict which was taking place.

Although I clearly remember anticipating the invasion of Britain, and week by week heard both in my own village and at my own school the latest casualties and heartbreaks, I never for one moment believed that Hitler would not be defeated. My prayers were always based upon the final triumph of an almighty God whose love was as great as his power.

My early links with the church were very basic. I often pumped the bellows for the organ at chapel, somewhat self-righteously giving the sixpence I earned back. On cold winter Sunday mornings I would get up to light the church boiler. In the quietness of the early morning I would linger in the church to pray. My early encounters with Jesus were both real and exciting. They were intensely personal and I once even had a vision of him which has remained with me all my life. Jesus ceased to be a model and became a mentor. Jesus sprang from the pages of history into my everyday life. I laughed with him. I wept with him. I was aware of his presence as I went to sleep and the moment I awoke. My life was inextricably bound up with his presence. I soon recognised that if I really did listen to God silently I would hear him speak. Almost invariably he spoke to me about tangible matters of immediate importance – matters of the day. Jesus became very much an all-knowing companion – the one with whom I could share my innermost secrets.

The hymns which I sang in the little chapel where I worshipped became part of my life, they expressed graphically the nature of God. As I sang these I shared a deep and growing love for the Jesus of history. As I began to read the writings of the saints, I sensed a great oneness with them and a growing intimacy with Jesus. He taught me about the bonds of love. He enabled me to understand compassion and forgiveness. He also implanted in my heart a deep anger and sadness in the face of unfairness and injustice.

Good Friday was always a hard day for me. It all seemed so wrong and I never ceased to be staggered at the folly of humankind shrieking for the release of Barabbas and sending my Jesus to the cross.

After the war I saw a cartoon in a national newspaper. It depicted the dark mushroom of an atomic bomb being exploded and this mushroom cast its sombre shadow across the face of the earth. This shadow took the form of a cross and I began to understand that all the important aspects of the life of our Lord need to be seen and even experienced at the present moment. I began to realise that each time a child died of starvation, Jesus was being crucified; but I also began to realise that every day could be Christmas Day with Jesus born afresh into our lives. I began to read the gospels in a new way. I began to understand the great urgency and the driving enthusiasm, not just of the evangelists and preachers who I had heard and met, but of the early church itself. I was struck with the basic simplicity of the gospel.

My prayer life developed very rapidly as I read the gospel stories in the present tense. I soaked up the writings of men like Thomas à Kempis like blotting paper. I hammered on God's doors when I was confronted with human suffering and pain. My encounter with Jesus became very dynamic and often quite stormy. I would talk to Jesus, I would question him very closely, I even found myself rebuking him and disagreeing with him and then feeling very sorry. In all this wrestling it became apparent to me that either the gospel of Jesus was all-consuming and of supreme value and importance, or it meant absolutely nothing.

The more time I spent in prayer, the more uneasy I became about aspects of Church and national life. I believed that God was calling for renewal of faith in the life of the Church and at the tender age of fifteen I began to preach with passion born of an ever closer encounter with Jesus as my Saviour and friend.

Although in my teens I was a comparatively lonely Christian, I was very deeply conscious of being part of the living body of Christ – closely bonded to the men of faith, in the Bible, in the history of the church, and today. God gave me a great burden in the Church and I fervently prayed for the mighty wind of the Holy Spirit to move among churches throughout the land.

It was years later that I, as a nonconformist, leapt for joy when that good Pope opened the windows of the Vatican to allow the Holy Spirit to blow in and produce the exciting vision of Vatican II.

The same convictions about my country and the world impelled me into politics. I was confronted with a Jesus whose gospel called for a total and radical change in me, in all people and in the world. I, therefore, entered politics with a burning zeal and grew to understand more fully the nature of my Methodist inheritance with its equal emphasis upon personal holiness and social righteousness. I could see little distinction between the pulpit in church and the political platform.

My involvement in politics and campaigning on social issues had a fundamental affect on my prayer life. I would wrestle in prayer about complex issues where God's will was not, at first, discernible. Increasingly, my prayers were specific to immediate situations and individual people with whom I was involved. In terms of injustice God taught me, not only how to pray for the victims, but for the perpetrators. I asked questions in prayer and received answers. I asked for confirmation of these answers and I consistently received this information, often from the most unexpected sources. Prayer became a ceaseless activity. I would address meetings and in the silence of my heart I would pray for all those present. I would read my newspaper and pray for those featured in the various stories. I would go to church and pray specifically for the preacher and the congregation. I even prayed for the writers of the many books which I read.

In all these prayers I came into a deeper knowledge of basic incarnational theology. I grew to understand the compassion and gentleness of Jesus. I grew to understand his forthrightness and anger. Often I would pray for God to bring into my life the people whom he wanted me to meet. My prayers to this end were answered in the most amazing way over many years as I travelled extensively throughout this country and abroad. I remember praying with my political opponents – far easier than I had originally anticipated. I found prayers for strangers particularly exhilarating. I prayed for the people I saw and sometimes spoke to on trains, in planes, on the underground and on the streets. In praying for them I developed a real love for the stranger.

As a comparatively young person I was led to Christian work among young people. For much of my married life my home was constantly filled with large numbers of teenagers and young adults. Through them I repeatedly experienced the freshness and joy of new-found faith and the exhilaration of those discovering the presence of the Lord in their lives. I shared with them their frustrations at what seemed to be deadness at the heart of much institutional religion. With them I was repeatedly reminded that Jesus was not the staid figure of history depicted by some religious people – He was in some ways a fiery revolutionary, a living and disturbing influence challenging our whole approach to life.

Both in preaching and youth work I frequently met fierce opposition and I was deeply wounded by this, but

God consistently led me back to the great prophets of the Old Testament for encouragement and inspiration.

I increasingly realised that God wanted to breathe the fire of his life-giving Spirit into the dry bones which were so apparent in both the churches and society. I also realised that any change had to start with me because, although I was aware of the solution, I was in fact part of the problem.

Youthful and often immature faith prepared the way for a new experience of the awesomeness of God and of his transcendent power and glory. In addition to walking with him as a friend I had to prostrate myself before him in utter lowliness and humility. Repeatedly over the years God reminded me of the futility of the whole worldly process of seeking power and success. I was particularly struck by the simplicity of St Francis and especially moved by the writing and lifestyle of Carlo Carretto, one of the Little Brothers of Charles de Foucauld. In praying with him I learnt that I had to become small and weak. My future walk with God was not to be in the wealth and security of industry or in the power of politics, but in the simplicity of a little child. Jean Vanier reminded me that Jesus is to be found at the bottom of the ladder of success – not the top. There we meet him with and in the poor and the rejected.

More recently, I was led into a spiritual desert where, bereft of home, family and possessions and all the props of life, I was alone with God. The desert was far removed from the noise, dirt and squalor of the world. It was lonely and there was a profound stillness. I was naked before his all-seeing gaze and in the wilderness silence I heard him speak. His words were simple and affirming. They gave purpose and value to my life. Above all, my eyes became fixed upon him rather than on myself.

My life, then, has been a pilgrimage during which, year by year, God has unfolded new truths and broadened horizons. I have always felt myself held in his arms as a little child. He is in a real sense, my Father, and my meeting with God in Jesus has become so close that I can truly feel his breath upon my life and receive his Spirit.

Throughout my adult life, as I have reached out and shared with people in prayer, I have seen his powerful Spirit at work. I can testify to the healing touch of Jesus in the lives of vast numbers of people I have encountered and in my own life. Amid all the uncertainties of life I can rejoice that God's liberating love never ceases. In the face of setback, sorrow and tribulation his goodness and mercy know no end.

When all else falls, he stands supreme, towering over the wrecks of time. Whatever happens, Jesus is the Lord of my life and the Lord of all creation.

HOPE AMID CHANGE AND INADEQUACY

Paul Hypher

Paul Hypher has worked in parishes for thirty-four years and is currently parish priest of Newmarket in Suffolk. He is also a commissioner for schools and a member of the Bishops' Conference Committee for Other Faiths. He is actively involved in justice and peace issues, and in the management of St Theresa's House, a day centre for needy and homeless people in Peterborough. Paul is currently doing postgraduate studies in sacramental theology and the theology of ministry.

Paul Hypher concludes the foregoing personal testimonies by setting them as it were against a theological background. His own personal testimony to God's healing presence in life is touched on through these words from his abbreviated contribution: 'Sacrament conveys to us the nature and power of God in such a way as to release God's power within us, changing us, so that we seek to live differently.' The mantle of St Francis, in his humility and commitment to the poor, seems to have fallen upon Monsignor Paul in these our times, as we see when we ponder especially his final paragraph.

K.O'S.

It is said of St Francis of Assisi that he had a deep and perpetual sense of the power of the Holy Spirit pervading everything – trees, animals, people, rocks, mountains, sky – much as one might sense the depths of a human person by looking into their eyes. What a gift! What a prompting to prayer!

Yet very many of us have been gifted with a similar mystical experience, however brief, perhaps just once or twice in our lives. Adults whose lives are shaped by purpose and moral conviction have almost invariably had some spiritual experience of this sort.

It may have been an overwhelming conviction of an utter oneness, meaning, and presence in and through the created world. We may have had an overwhelming sense, perhaps briefly, that created things are just the mantle of a deeper reality that is far more intense than we can grasp or imagine.

Our experience may have come through knowing or working with someone whose life reflected a deep spiritual awareness and moral probity – a member of the family, a stranger, someone who was alongside us in a time of pain or disaster.

An experience like this may have quite simply taken us by surprise. Or perhaps the ground was laid by a disciplined stillness at the centre point of our being. However it was, such experiences are always sheer gift, never contrived or manipulated.

We may treasure such moments for the rest of our lives.

Every detail of where we were, what we were hearing, what we were seeing can remain very firmly embedded in our mind's eye. The memories may resurface again and again to renew us; they may summon us to rediscover meaning not only in times of joy and peace, but often, and perhaps especially, in suffering, failure, depression and even sin.

Sometimes sadly we take little notice of such promptings of the Spirit, or we even consign them to a previous naïve period in our lives.

The Church has a word for such interactions between deepest reality and our innermost selves which take place in and through experience of created things and events. That word is 'sacrament'.

Sacrament conveys to us the nature and power of God in such a way as to release God's power within us, changing us so that we seek to live differently. Sacrament is fundamental to our relationship to God. God communicates with us only in ways in which it is possible for us to receive and experience his love and sense something of the mystery at the unutterable depths of his being. There is no other way. In our relationship with ultimate reality, with God, everything is symbol, everything is sacrament.

Everything and everyone can speak to us of the inner reality of God, of God's relationship to us and of our relationship to God so as to bring that deepest reality into our lives. Equally everything and everyone can only ever be utterly inadequate in speaking to us about God's relationship to us and our relationship to God.

God speaks to us through nature, through the Scriptures, through the prophets and through the story and the rites and customs of his people. God speaks to us most especially through Jesus. God speaks to us through the history of the Church, through its tradition, creeds and teachings, through the lives of the saints and the writings, icons, sculptures and buildings of his people. God speaks to us through the courage of martyrs, the selfless service of ministers and the faithfulness of ordinary people. God speaks through the devotion of those who seek God in their hearts, the gut compassion of those who care, and the integrity of those who fight for justice. God speaks through the simplicity of the faith of children and the serenity of the dying. All of these things are sacraments of the presence of God's Holy Spirit.

The preacher's words too are sacrament. They may be eloquent and clever or boring and ill-formed. Whatever they are they are inadequate to express the true nature of God's mystery. Yet they still have the power in the most surprising of ways to be instruments of the Spirit in transforming the hearts of listeners.

In the sacraments the community of the Church re-enacts, in symbol and gesture and in mutual and prayerful relationship to God and in relationship to those called to share in the sacrament, the meaning of God's love, the salvation offered us in Christ and the way in which these are at work in the day-to-day lives of people and of the Church.

Both the indispensability of sacrament in which God speaks and its inadequacy are important. Without sacrament we cannot know God, but without its utter inadequacy we are tempted to worship the sign rather than the infinite reality that it manifests. All sacraments without exception are inadequate in this way – nature, rite, doctrinal formulation, the Church, the community and indeed human love.

More profoundly, the very inadequacy of sacrament touches something at the very heart of the Godhead; for darkness is not simply a negation of light but in a way darkness can give light meaning. God's strength comes to full power in and through our weakness.

If then we allow this continual inadequacy to frustrate us, make us dissatisfied or lose hope, rather than lead us to stand silent before the mystery, we close the paths to life and growth.

We close the paths to life in many ways. We can close our eyes and hearts to what God is doing in sacrament by being bored, or too self-preoccupied. We can close our hearts to what God is doing by insisting that God's Spirit is only at work in circumstances which fit our preconceptions of perfection, or by highlighting the shortcomings or lack of integrity of those in whom God is at work. We can close our hearts by giving vent to anger and prejudice ('nothing good ever comes out of Nazareth').

We can even close our eyes and hearts to what God is doing by allowing the shattering of our justified dreams and by allowing our experiences of injustice to fill us with the kind of disappointment that destroys hope. We can close our eyes and hearts to what God is doing by allowing shortcomings and even sinfulness in the Church, whether institutional and official, or local and parochial, to smother for us any perception of the faith, goodness and integrity that are also there.

St Francis experienced God in and through all reality. He grasped the radical nature of Jesus' call to be in solidarity with the poor and the way in which the Spirit enables Jesus to be present. He understood well the corruption and misplaced power of the Church of his time. Whatever disappointment, disillusion or anger was his, his sense of the sacramentality of the Church enabled him both to grasp the mystery and to cope with the Church's inadequacy, to challenge its shortcomings and to work in love through the symbol of the rebuilding of Portiuncula for the rebuilding of the whole Church.

A COMING TOGETHER

Kathleen O'Sullivan

Kathleen O'Sullivan was for many years headmistress of a Dublin high school but after taking early retirement she devoted herself to the study of spirituality. She has written A Way of Life, Light out of Darkness *and* God's Delight, *and has been very active in making the prayer life described in those books a reality in the lives of many people. She has now handed on most of those responsibilities but she continues to write, to serve as a spiritual director and to listen, to discern God's plans for the future.*

As I read the individual contributions in this book and, most especially, when I read right through them all I was deeply moved and filled with the power of the Holy Spirit that emanated from them. For me, it was a sacred, sacramental experience.

I was aware of an inflow of life from the Spirit – like a baptismal renewal; the honest, trusting sharing of one writer following the other was like the sacrament of communion, yet in the laying down of their life, in and through the power of Christ, it was eucharistic. The sharing with writers who had been deeply drawn into repentance and renewal was as the sacrament of reconciliation, where, vicariously, we too came to know anew the intimacy of wholeness in Christ. The inner strength of each individual who had moved closer into Christ was like the laying-on-of-hands as in the sacrament of confirmation.

This is the Church of Christ. This is how we, the body of Christ, with Christ our head, build his Church together. It is a question of letting the risen Christ become incarnate, each moment, within us, so that our **life-experience** becomes the life of Christ alive within us; this is truly the fullness of life – his own life – which he promised to give us. Thus his own words are fulfilled: 'I am the way, the truth and the life' (John 14:6). Whatever, therefore, we may find *life-giving* in the writers' accounts of their finding Jesus in their life-experience, flows to us, from the presence of Jesus with them, as they recalled and wrote.

We are the Church; we say that we love Christ, that we want to centre on him and not on ourselves. From testimonies which we have read, we see that being self-centred brings us into debilitating darkness, but trusting in Christ brings us into the light. The more we acknowledge our darkness and come to Christ for healing, the more we become the living Church; then we are empowered to become one with God and one with our neighbour. The fulfilment of his own prayer to the Father for us delights the heart of Christ: 'I pray that all of them may be one, Father, just as you are in me and I am in you. May they also be in us so that the world may believe that you have sent me' (John 17:20–2).

Belief in Christ is what we, the world, need, if in all things we are to be nourished in faith – belief in Christ, belief in his mission of love to save us, belief that we are God's children precious to him, belief that in being his Church we are bonded in his love and life as brothers and sisters. **Our faith today has weakened**; consequently our hope in God and in one another has weakened, and love for God and for our neighbour has become devalued and debased.

We need to be aware of the 'roaring lion' but focused confidently on Christ the rock; we need to be aware of the voice of Christ speaking our name, calling us gently to be alert. He calls us to restore the Church of God that we are. We must begin with the quality of our personal love-response to him and – consequently – to our neighbour. Whenever I do the slightest kindness, stretch a helping hand, offer a listening heart to another person, Christ takes it as done to himself. When I then pause, give God time and listen, I will eventually recognise the sound of his voice. His voice is usually gentle in its approach, quite unexpected, surprising in myriad ways, alerting us sometimes when it appears to be the least convenient time for the one listening! *Ambassadors for Christ*, as we are all called to be, need to develop a deep sensitivity in recognising the voice of the one who sends them.

One thing is certain. The Spirit of God plumbs the depths of our hearts and reads them correctly. If our faith and hope and love of God is genuine, the Spirit cannot be deceived. If we listen and continue to listen and wait for God's time, he will speak. That is certain. Our weaknesses are not the barrier – because God has promised us the gift of his Spirit who prays for us to help us overcome those weaknesses, as St Paul tells us (Romans 8:26–7). *Barriers* are to be discovered and brought to God for dismantling. Let him remove our lack of forgiveness for one another and take from us our hard, selfish and self-centred hearts. We need the gift of wisdom to learn how to be truly dependent on God and not on ourselves. We pray for humility to help us understand the role of justice, to care for one another, to recognise that what we have freely received is intended to be shared with others, and so much more that the voice of God will teach the listening heart.

Faith and hope and love ensure sound, healthy relationships with God, with one another and with our self. The most important relationship that binds the human and the spiritual together is **prayer**, the personal relationship with God.

Prayer, properly understood, ensures our living in **reality**. Prayer is a relationship with God where we talk to God about the realities of who we are, about our life-situation, our weaknesses and fears, temptations and hopes. This **real** me reaches out to meet the **real** God, not through the head only but through the whole person that I am; I learn how to become familiar with movements of the Spirit, about discerning what is of God, what is of disturbing spirits and what is of my own frailty. All this helps me to avoid make-believe in the relationship with God. Since prayer takes seriously my relationship with other people, then prayer is the way to become **real** with other people as well as with God. This is when **worship** – individually or communally – becomes truly the praise and glory of God, offered by his body.

The sad thing about us as Church today is that *prayer*

is too often seen as a duty; saying words by rote, or even saying psalms, or attending Mass, but too often *without the living faith* that allows the Spirit of God to bring about a meeting of the whole person – body, mind, heart and spirit – with almighty God.

Without becoming people of prayer, people who are at ease with our God, as Father, as Saviour and as the indwelling Spirit, we miss out on the joy of being human, the joy of letting Christ live within us always; we miss out on hearing his voice and therefore on building his Church together.

Practically everyone who has contributed to this book has been influenced by leading, or participating in retreats or groups based on *Light out of Darkness*. I mention this as an outstanding example of how the Church was built by the body of Christ, God's people. Twenty years ago, a very small group of people, thirsting for God, asked me, a stranger to England, to help them. They told me that they thirsted for the real God who would not be just a Sunday God; they also knew they needed to get support from one another and they also felt that if they were to come to know the **real** God, they needed to know their **real** selves.

A book, entitled *A Way of Life*, answered their needs in large measure, followed some years later by *Light out of Darkness*. The important point, however, is this: those people who truly **thirsted** and sought help were the *instruments of the Spirit* to get God's work done. They were ambassadors for Christ! They pointed me in the right direction. They openly declared their need and together we journeyed. I shared the skills I had, but their eagerness and fidelity – with the resulting transformation of their lives – was the necessary confirmation given me by God.

Nor is that all, some have continued on this same journey for nearly two decades and now have taken over from me, releasing me for writing and new ministries – all because they themselves took action in their thirst for God; others have moved into a variety of ministries in various parishes, spreading the harvest in different ways. And now, with this new book, *Ambassadors for Christ*, it is as if a third generation has taken up the challenge to keep rebuilding the Church of God by sharing their faith story with a wider audience. And it all began with the sowing of a very small seed!

No wonder I keep finding riches in Isaiah 55, where the prophet seems to be speaking of *our* little experience:

> Come all you who are thirsty
> Come to the waters . . .
> Listen, listen to me, and eat what is good,
> And your soul will delight in the richest of fare
> Give ear and come to me;
> Hear me that your soul may live . . .
> Seek the Lord while he may be found;
> Call on him while he is near . . .
> For my thoughts are not your thoughts,
> Neither are your ways my ways

> (Isa. 55:1, 2–3, 6, 8)

Later, the verses bring us into touch with the voice of the Lord and the power of the *word* that he speaks:

> . . . my word that goes out from my mouth
> will not return to me empty,
> but will accomplish what I desire

and achieve the purpose for which I sent it.

(Isa. 55:11)

Finally, we recognise what happens when we hear the voice of the Lord and listen to the word despite preliminary resistance – as I experienced initially when God seemed to ask for this present book. Once again, the body of Christ, by their wholehearted response, was the ambassadorial *instrument* used by God to confirm that it was truly his voice that I had heard, when it seemed to me that he was asking the impossible at a most inconvenient time! (I had still much work to do to complete my previous work, *God's Delight*.)

> You will go out in joy
> and be led forth in peace;
> the mountains and the hills
> will burst into song before you,
> and all the trees of the field
> will clap their hands.
> Instead of the thorn bush will grow the pine tree,
> and instead of briars the myrtle will grow.
> This will be for the Lord's renown,
> for an everlasting sign,
> which will not be destroyed.

(Isa. 55:12–13)

As God's people, his Church, may we stay awake to hear his voice and be assured in faith, that whatever God begins, he completes, 'carrying us every step of the way' (Deut. 1:31). Thus he forms his ambassadors.

AMBASSADORS FOR CHRIST

Within us, united with him, may the voice of the Lord keep resounding. In the power of God, may the blessed Trinity be adored and worshipped, now and for ever by us, his Church, that is his body.